The Homeowner's Guide to
LIVING IN
FRANCE

More related titles

Buying a Property in France
An insider guide to realising your dream

'Honest, independent advice you can't do without when buying a property in France.' — French Property News

Buying and Renovating a Property in France

All the practical advice and information you need to make your purchase and renovation of an older house in France a pleasure and not a chore.

Going to Live in France
Your practical guide to life and work in France

'An in-depth insight… Gives the reader a real taste, whether property buyer, student, business person or tourist.' — Making Money

Starting and Running a B&B in France
How to make money and enjoy a new lifestyle running your own chambres d'hôtes

'Author and B&B owner Deborah Hunt reveals what you need to succeed.' — French Magazine

howtobooks
Send for a free copy of the latest catalogue to:
How To Books
3 Newtec Place, Magdalen Road,
Oxford OX4 1RE, United Kingdom
email: info@howtobooks.co.uk
http://www.howtobooks.co.uk

The Homeowner's Guide to
LIVING IN
FRANCE

RICHARD WHITING

howtobooks

Published by How To Books Ltd,
3 Newtec Place, Magdalen Road,
Oxford, OX4 1RE, United Kingdom
Tel: (01865) 793806 Fax: (01865) 248780
email: info@howtobooks.co.uk
http://www.howtobooks.co.uk

First edition 2005

British Library Cataloguing in Publication Data
A catalogue record for this book is available from
the British Library.

Produced for How To Books by Deer Park Productions, Tavistock
Typeset by *specialist* publishing services ltd, Milton Keynes
Printed and bound by Bell & Bain Ltd, Glasgow

Note: The material contained in this book is set out in good
faith for general guidance and no liability can be accepted
for loss or expense incurred as a result of relying in particular
circumstances on statements made in the book. The laws and
regulations are complex and liable to change, and readers should
check the current position with the relevant authorities before
making personal arrangements.

Contents

Part 2 Living in France

Preface

France is consistently the world's top tourist destination, with around 75 million visitors annually. France is always news for the British although our tabloid press often give it shoddy treatment.

In April 2004 the Queen carried out a rare state visit to France to commemorate the centenary of the *Entente Cordiale*, having officially launched (in Southampton) the French-built *Queen Mary 2* liner a few months earlier.

Property is noticeably cheaper in France and the cost of living, including food, is somewhat cheaper, the weather is better than in the UK and the social security and health systems are among the best in the world.

Having lived and worked in France for the last 20 years after over 30 years in the UK I have tried in this book to lay out my experience and understanding of France, the French and the French way of life. I hope to help permanent residents, frequent visitors and those with second homes in France, and also would-be first- or second-home owners, to get the best out of France and discover often overlooked but important aspects of it: all at correct prices. What to do, and not to do, if you want to be liked or at least accepted, *and* pitfalls to avoid are also themes in *The Homeowner's Guide to Living in France*.

This guide selectively considers themes behind pre-conceived ideas. My wife, Nicole, is French and was brought up in Algeria until her family came to live in France in 1962 when Algeria gained its independence. As a French national who has had to adapt to living in France and as a state school teacher for nearly 40 years she has been a remarkable source of information. I would also like to thank in particular

Antoine Peretti, *Docteur en Sciences Humaines* and employed by the *l'Education Nationale*, whose suggestions for Chapter 10 were extremely helpful.

The French are perfectionists. Second best often won't do. They are quick to criticise and complain if anything falls just short of expectations. As a result, many of the good things in France are undoubtedly the best in the world. Even when the best is achieved without a shadow of a doubt, like winning football's World Cup against Brazil in 1998, questions may be asked. 'Was skulduggery or double-dealing involved?' Or 'How did we (France) manage to…?' The means to the end also has to be supreme. The art has to be there. I have spoken to a winning weekend amateur tennis player who, having trounced his opponent 6–0, received suggestions from the *loser* on how he (the winner) could improve his game!

Bureaucracy, on the other hand is another matter. Napoleon, more than a perfectionist, laid the foundations 200 years ago of French bureaucracy. Twenty per cent of the working population are civil or public servants. The enormous draw-back is that bureaucratic systems have become so sophisticated and complicated that simple official requests may take days, even weeks, to be processed through different channels. For example, a visit to the post office, if you're not armed with at least your ID, is not recommended although you can now send a registered letter through the post office by email.

Part One of this book, Setting the Scene, gives a background to France. There are chapters on France's natural beauty and places considered to offer the most attractive life-styles; French family life; the economy, politics and future developments and buying a property (existing or on-plan, and the diversity of house and apartment types).

Part Two, Living in France, covers topics such as day-to-day practical life (health, language, integrating socially, shopping); leisure activities; holidays in France; culture; education; employment; business dealings; eating out (with regional specialities) including up-to-date and lesser known possibilities.

New French words encountered in the text, and some words you are likely to come across, are found at the end of each topic or chapter in a useful vocabulary panel.

Some French words will be used for which there is no real UK equivalent. From *baguette* to *bidet*, *château* to *cuisine* and *bon appetit!*: French stick, cooking, castle and enjoy your meal! won't do. *Bon appetit!*, for example, is a nice way for the host to indicate that everyone has been served and that the serious business of eating can start: much more elegant than 'tuck in!' and more meaningful today than grace.

While reliable sources provide the prices and figures in the text they should always be treated as approximate. Prices should be verified at the precise moment when an important buying decision is being made.

Useful Websites and Further Reading appendices complement the overall information and to avoid embarrassing misunderstandings, there is also a table of Some False Friends, listing some of the most commonly encountered words in French – with their precise meanings – which look or sound like English words, but which do not have the same meanings.

Richard Whiting

PART ONE

SETTING THE SCENE

1
The Beauty of France

The country

Affectionately known to its people as the *héxagone,* France starts – going westwards from an English standpoint – with the English Channel (*La Manche,* which has no reference to England). It runs along to the Atlantic followed by a left turn down the Bay of Biscay, turning left again across the Pyrenees, left along the Mediterranean coast, left up through the Southern French Alps and the Savoy Alps and finally skirting left round the European seat of Parliament in Strasbourg onto the penultimate side of its hexagon outline along the German, Luxembourg and Belgian borders running up to the Calais area.

It is the largest country in Europe, over twice as large as the UK, with around the same population of just over 60 million. There are still endless areas of unspoilt countryside and long natural beaches – particularly on the Atlantic coast – to be enjoyed. Its Atlantic, Channel and Mediterranean coastlines, coupled with the Pyrenees, Alps, Massif Central highlands and inland Continental plains account for distinctive climatic zones. There are huge temperature differences between Mediterranean and Continental climatic zones in winter – and sometimes huge temperature variations within the same area during the same day. The absolute record for temperature variation throughout the same day in one place is attributed to an area in the north of the Massif Central with a variation of 40° centigrade – just over 100° Fahrenheit – on a summer day in 1885. Mountainous areas are of course often subject to sudden changes in the weather. British readers might note that the Cévennes area, which is very sparsely populated, on the south-eastern edge of the Massif Central in southern France, is reckoned to be the wettest area. The landscape in France is probably the most varied in Europe with the Atlantic lowlands and Continental lowlands running from the Loire to the Vosges area, hilly areas mainly to the north of the French Alps, the Alps and the Pyrenees, and the sub-Alps mountainous areas in parts of the South of France and Corsica. Following the *Tour de France* on television throughout July gives an armchair-view of France.

Communications

France is ideally situated for travel to northern, southern and central Europe. Its internal *TGV* high-speed train network (the *TGV* train is undoubtedly the best locomotive in the world) is expanding all the time and the multiple lane motorway network is a joy to drive on. Low-cost, no frills airlines are keeping down the price of tickets from traditional passenger airlines like Air France and British Airways and, increasingly, flights to cities outside France are offered by local as well as regional airports. Bergerac airport in the Dordogne area, which is immensely popular with the British, now offers regular budget flights. UK executives can work in Britain during the week and enjoy their French home at weekends. Parisians using the three-hour *TGV* connection to Marseille can and do now live in Provence at the weekend.

France's people

Ethnically, France is a rich, colourful mix. Approximately seven per cent of the working population are immigrants. Between 1999 and 2002 there was an increase of 36 per cent overall in the number of foreign national immigrants. Portuguese nationals hold the record for the number of immigrants to France from a European country. There are Europeans of various extractions; Africans originating from francophone West African countries such as Cameroon, The Ivory Coast and Senegal; people from the overseas territories of the Polynesian islands and New Caledonia – the *TOM (Territoires Outre-Mer)* – and overseas *départements* of Guadeloupe, Martinique, French Guyana and the Réunion – the *DOM (Départements Outre-Mer)*; Arabs; Berbers from the former North African protectorates of Morocco and Tunisia and the former *département* of Algeria; Madagascans; and descendants from the old territories of French Indo-China. Apart from the advantages that this multi-ethnic society has brought, not least to the realm of French gastronomic expertise (see Chapter 13), in recent years France has successfully exported to the UK, albeit for personal taxation reasons, some of their top sporting talent with ethnic origins. The English Premier League football clubs are not complaining.

While French nationals and the French language are classified as Latin, Britanny is proudly Celt and it still has its own language which is like Welsh. The Alsace and Lorraine areas are still, rather reluctantly, impregnated with the Germanic legacy of the 1870 Franco-Prussian war. The Côte d'Azur's real natives among its cosmopolitan population could still be in Italy, as the area was until 1860. The people of south-west France bear a strong imprint from neighbouring Spain.

Such a kaleidoscopic mixture inevitably leads to a certain empathy between people of the same origin. All things being equal, '*pieds-noirs*', the French brought up in Algeria who have a reputation for being particularly dynamic and hard-working, prefer to deal in practical matters with fellow '*pieds-noirs*'. Laid-back, proud Corsicans definitely like to deal with Corsicans. Armenians whose genocide in Turkey in 1915 was only officially recognised as such by France a few years ago will go out of their way to discuss business with a 'Kaloustian', 'Aznavourian' or other '…ian'. Alsatians (*Alsaciens*) – not to be confused with Armenians – have been voted the friendliest people in France while Mediterraneans from Marseille to Nice are often regarded, quite unjustifiably, by northern French people as indolent and unreliable people basking in the sun. The people from the Auvergne central region are said to appreciate the value of money: a sou is a sou.

Defining indefinable *chic*

Chic is the very essence of the attraction so many people have for France. But what is it? Is it definable? There are at least 14 French magazines devoted to fashion (*mode*) from *Biba* to *Vogue*, regional newspapers with fashion and trends (*tendances*) features, articles and supplements. Property magazines also have features on new high-tech designer products which have no real connection with property interiors and there are numerous interior decoration magazines: is '*chic*' style and design as well? 'Design' is now part of the French language while 20 years ago it wasn't in the French dictionary. A product may be the best on the market, but if it doesn't look modern unless it's deliberately 'retro', is too classic in appearance, doesn't conform to the '*tendance*' for colour and 'look' (also a recent addition to the French dictionary) it won't be successful. *Chic* may shock. Brown refrigerators were popular in the 1980s. Yellow or red men's jackets were popular in the 1990s.

Chic has become more international. The Italians, always masters of industrial design, are more prevalent on the French marketplace. So is IKEA, the Swedish furniture manufacturer, designer and retailer which has somewhat ousted Terence Conran's Habitat stores. In recent years English fashion designers, heading up artistic departments of leading French fashion houses, have become more *avant-garde* than the French themselves.

The French realise that *chic* now requires more than using natural artistic flair for short haircuts, having natural dress sense and walking sexily, or its secondary meaning of being decent and honest. The translated modern-day primary meaning (taken from the *Robert* dictionary) 'the ease of doing something elegantly' is no longer sufficient. *Nouvelle cuisine*, which came into fashion 20 years ago because eating attractively and well-prepared food in small portions was original and *chic*, no longer has much of a following. *Chic* cannot rest on its laurels and has evolved to *tendances* (trends) to keep pace with consumers' requirements.

How the French eat

Eating and drinking habits, the importance given to each meal and healthy eating are essential to the French way of life. Food accounts for the greatest part of family expenditure, exceeding repayments on property purchase or accommodation rent. The *Sunday Times* wrote in 1955: '…French children are expected to eat like adults and English people to eat like their children'. French parents still try to impose this thinking but will now give in from time to time to the demand for fish fingers or hamburgers and chips from young children. Eating out, restaurant categories and regional specialities are discussed in Chapter 13.

Eating habits in France have changed over the last 20 years for busy executives (*cadres*) who don't have time to go home for lunch. They are prepared to stand up or sit in sandwich bars or eat hamburgers in fast-food restaurants as long as they do actually eat. There is no real translation of *Bon appetit!* in English. In France a business appointment or casual encounter with an acquaintance which finishes around 11.30 am will gain points with this salutation. It might even get you a free lunch! Some offices actually close between 12 (*midi*) and 2 pm (*14h*) and most independent shops which are not in shopping centres (*centres commerciaux*) close between these meal hours. Meal times (*heures de repas*) confirm their importance in private For Sale (*A Vendre*) notices and advertisements for cars, houses, etc. *Heures de repas* abbreviated to HR follows the home telephone number. Potential buyers are thus almost certain they will be able to speak to sellers, even if they both have mouths full of food!

Blue-collar workers and lorry drivers religiously respect the lunch break during the working week and their unions make sure that an adequate period with suitable expenses is allowed for people on the road '*en déplacement*' to have a sit-down three-course meal. It was also interesting to see during a TV property conversion series on the M6 channel, involving teams of DIY competitors, that at least two competitors every day were seconded, straight after breakfast, to the on-site kitchen to prepare lunch for everybody.

Meal-time drinks

Tighter application of the drink-drive regulations since the right-wing government was elected in April 2002 has seen a marked decrease in wine consumption in France. Bottled water consumption with meals has doubled in recent years. Vineyard proprietors are also suffering from increased imports of quality wines from Chile, California, Australia and South Africa. 'Drink better wine' is the cry, knowing that the consumption of wine is unlikely to increase. The whole wine classification (*appellation*) labelling system is under review by wine-growers' associations to see if the virtues of individual French wines can be shown on the bottle more simply. All good news for the customer.

The pre-lunch weekday *apéritif* is increasingly rare unless a business lunch with colleagues has been organised and somebody has opted to act as chauffeur and have no more than one *apéritif* and one glass of wine with the meal. Many restaurants now offer wine by the glass, like English pubs, as an alternative to varying carafe (*pichet*) sizes of house wine and some give wine-bottle take-away bags so you can finish a good bottle of wine at home. End of the week (or term if you are a teacher) early evening *apéritifs* are popular. An *apéritif* is a must before any formal or informal dinner party. An evening *apéritif dinatoire* is exactly what it suggests. Evening drinks with hot and/or cold buffet food, such as pizzas, quiches and savouries, ending probably with a dessert and possibly champagne: a dinner in itself. Cheese and wine parties are no comparison. An invitation to dine at someone's home is, as it should be, a serious matter. My wife and I turned up once for an informal dinner with friends who had completely forgotten about the invitation. No question of rustling up some food. We were whisked off to their local restaurant, and it was the first and only time I've eaten frogs' legs (*cuisses de grenouille*), thighs actually, in 20 years in France.

Children's food

Young children are not overlooked. While 'elevenses' are not part of the school curriculum, after all lunch is at 12 o'clock, youngsters leaving school around 4pm are immediately given the *goûter* (after-school snack of soft drink and biscuits) in their Mum's or minder's car on the way home. They will of course be eating the evening meal with the rest of the family.

Visiting the top sights of France

- As a priority, visit the centre of Paris and use it as a base for visiting the grandiose châteaux of Versailles and the Loire valley and the stunning Mont-St-Michel abbey in Normandy.

- Fly or drive 550 miles from Paris (900 kms) to Nice as your base for touring in the South of France, taking in the sophisticated Principality of Monaco, classy and expensive Cannes and then going inland and westwards to traditional Provence and the charming town of Aix-en-Provence. The southern ambiance, not least the weather, is quite unlike the Paris area, another country. (If you're driving, avoid the motorway through Lyon over extended holiday weekends and in the spring and summer holiday seasons. It is a notorious bottleneck.)

- After that the choice is yours between say Britanny, the French Alps and picturesque Alsace.

- History buffs should also visit the Gallo-Roman vestiges west of the Rhône valley and the beautifully preserved medieval fortress town of Carcassonne.

See also page 165 for details of France's 28 UNESCO World Heritage cultural and natural sites.

Where to live

Attractive towns

The places mentioned above are not necessarily the most attractive areas to live in, unless you like crowds all year round.

If you have been posted to a major town or city by your company, you may still have some choice as to where you live due to the extension of the TGV train network. For example Dijon, in the beautiful Burgundy wine region, is now more accessible to both Paris and Lyon. It is regularly near the top of the *Le Point* magazine's annual Best Towns to Live In in France rating and came second in the 2004 rating. The *Le Point* rating system takes into account town hall answers to questions on employment prospects, crime, road safety, demographic profile, cultural heritage, pollution and natural catastrophe risks, local economy, the housing situation (see Chapter 4 for indications of property prices throughout France), higher educational establishments, leisure possibilities and the general attractiveness of the town. Visit www.lepoint.fr (in French) at the beginning of each year for the latest table.

Some *Le Point* town ratings yo-yo over the years. Nantes, on the Atlantic coast, the fourth biggest port in France has, however, consistently been top, or near the top, in recent years. It was top in 2003 and in 2004. Montpellier, a dynamic progressive

Mediterranean city, and Chambéry, gateway to the Savoy ski resorts, are constantly in the top 20 (out of 100). Marseille has transformed its traditionally sinister image in recent years and shot up in the ratings.

Best areas

The *Le Point* survey and employment prospects apart, the Alpes de Haute Provence *département* is considered among the best areas in which to live in France. In summer this *département* has Mediterranean day-time temperatures, turning cooler with the evening mountain air. It offers hiking and water sports in summer and skiing in winter. It is relatively pollution free and has around 300 sunny days a year. Property is considerably cheaper than on the Provençal coast, just two hours' drive away, and there is a relaxed, honest, country ambiance.

From the extremes of rural simplicity to urban sophistication and subtle combinations between, France boasts a wide choice.

Useful vocabulary

apéritif dinatoire	buffet dinner
beur	person born in France whose parents are North African immigrants
branché	trendy/hip
cadre	executive
centres commerciaux	shopping centres (covered or outdoor)
cuisses de grenouille	frogs' legs
département	department (equivalent to UK county): 96 in France, including Corsica
France profonde	rural France
HR (heures de repas)	mealtimes
Midi	South of France
midi	noon
parcs nationaux	national parks
parcs naturels régionaux	regional nature reserves
pieds-noirs	French born in Algeria
Régions	administrative regions: 23 in France, including Corsica
tendance	trend
TGV (train à grande vitesse)	high-speed train

2
Family Life

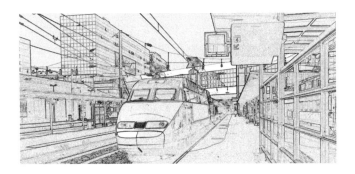

The breadwinners

Official school leaving age is 16 and retirement with full pension can be taken by working women and men at age 60 or even before in the public and private salaried sectors, provided certain conditions are met. This partly explains why in the 15–64 year-old age group in France 'only' 75 per cent of men and 62 per cent of women work as opposed to the UK's respective percentages of 83 per cent and 67 per cent.

Women have had the right to equal pay for identical work since 1983, but in practice the equal opportunities principle (and the resulting equal pay) is rarely applied in private commerce, manufacturing and service industries. With many primary and secondary schools closed on Wednesdays (and open on Saturday mornings) many women with children of school-age do not work on Wednesdays so, perhaps inevitably, tend to have less responsible positions. The 35-hour working week which applies now to most companies has, however, encouraged some couples, with both partners working, to divide Wednesdays between their work and children. For couples with pre-school aged children who do wish to work all week, France, like Scandinavian countries, has a much envied official child-care system with sliding scale income-related cost for day nurseries (*crèches*), kindergartens (*jardin d'enfants*) and qualified nannies offering small-group care.

Travelling to school and work

School

Urban areas provide bus passes for schoolchildren at reduced prices and rural communities, with limited bus services, lay on special school buses (*cars de ramassage scolaire*). Working mums often organise their office hours so that they can drop children off by car at school, at least in the mornings, with a friend or grandparent doing the honours after school. It is rare to see pupils walking a few kilometres to school and even cycling to school is decreasingly popular. The large cities of Lille, Lyon, Marseille, Toulouse and, of course, Paris, have *Métro* (Underground) trains and most recently Rennes (a smaller city with around 200,000 people) has too. The price for a ten-ticket *carnet* represents a huge saving on the cost of ten individual go-anywhere single journey tickets. Under ten-year-olds usually travel half-price.

Work

Public and civil servants (*fonctionnaires*) have regular fixed working hours and more often than not work in a town or city office with good day-time public transport (trains or buses). Salaried employees can have rail season tickets (*abonnements de travail*) by getting their employer's signature on the application form. Even on a weekly basis, these are extremely reasonable by comparison with UK rail network prices. They also work out much cheaper than travelling the same distance on the motorway and paying any toll-gate charges. Depending on the stretch of motorway, the toll charges can be as much as the price of fuel used. Part of this cost can be claimed against income tax liability if workers can show no reasonable alternative but to live more than 40 kms (25 miles) away from their work and that they have no choice other than using their car to go to and from work.

Other employees working irregular hours, shift-workers, executives who are expected by their employers to work more than the imposed 35-hour week, and people working in rural or suburban industrial trading estates go to work by car. Public transport time-tables, apart from town centre bus and *Métro* lines, and the Greater Paris suburban trains, do not really cater for working people outside the 8 am to 6 pm bracket. Trains are, however, punctual. A change-over in July 2004 to a new computerised ticket issuing system, which didn't work immediately and disrupted the national ticket purchase and reservation system for 24 hours, was quite exceptional.

The continually expanding *TGV* network has meant that people can now commute great distances at 300 kph (190 mph) to work on a daily or weekly basis. Commuting has become a new experience for many thousands of French people. In under 15 years Paris has been linked on dedicated high-speed track to the Atlantic coast (1989), to Lille (1993), to Lyon, the Channel Tunnel (1994) and to Marseille (2001). Non-smokers will be pleased to note that all *TGV* carriages (*voitures*) have been no-smoking since 2004.

The Air France season ticket card (*carte d'abonnement*) costs around 500€, giving holders up to 30 per cent discount on flight prices. Bear in mind that even with this discount, for example, the return flight price from Bordeaux or Toulouse to Paris is still around 300€, so *TGV* travel with similar door-to-door times is still a better deal.

Strikes

Rail strikes are nearly always notified in advance and a very limited service is guaranteed. Many commuters from the Paris suburbs may, however, decide to take a day off as the outer ring road (*périphérique*) and roads accessing it are absolute chaos. On a normal day the *périphérique* traffic grinds along between 15 and 20 kilometres an hour. Sharing cars (*co-voiturage*), walking hours to work, and cycling did though come into their own when there was virtually a general strike, which lasted some weeks, in the winter of 1995.

Every three or four years lorry drivers demand better pay or working conditions by reducing the number of motorway lanes open to traffic and blocking fuel pump deliveries. The backlog created on the motorways is, however, usually allowed to flow freely through the toll-gates – at no charge.

A day in the life of a family

This typical family lives in a medium sized town of 30,000 people 10 kms (6 miles) away from a regional conurbation with a population of around 250,000 people. Both parents work full-time and they have two children – the national average is around 1.8, vying with Ireland as the highest in Europe. The son goes to the university on the other side of the conurbation and the younger daughter now attends the local *lycée*, which is in the conurbation area.

The father works as a technical manager in a specialist small light engineering company (classed in France a *PME* or *PMI*: small- (*petite*) or medium- (*moyenne*) sized enterprise/industrial company) in one part of the conurbation and the mother works as a legal secretary in the town. None of the family works or studies near the others and starting and finishing times are not the same, so two cars, plus an older second-hand car and a scooter (scooters are in vogue again) are the simplest solution. They live in a small private estate (*lotissement privé*) in a one-garage three-bedroomed house with a good-sized but not large back garden. There is one bathroom and a small separate shower cubicle. There are a few outside designated parking spaces which are insufficient for all cars in the estate at the same time. Few people bother to garage their car overnight. At best one car and the scooter are behind a locked gate in the driveway, with the other two cars parked up on the pavement to ease the estate's traffic flow in the morning and evening rush hours.

Mum, dad and daughter start at 8.30 am so they're up at 6.30 am, which gives them all time to shower and have breakfast at a reasonable pace without tearing around the house. Breakfast during the week is a large bowl of percolated black coffee for the adults, hot chocolate, milk or fresh orange juice for the daughter, with baguette bread for everyone spread with butter or spooned (knives are definitely out) with dollops of jam from the back of a spoon. A bowl of cereal is more likely to be eaten by the women, who take starting the day with the right food more seriously than men. The student son, whose first lecture is not until 9.30 am, is gently yanked out of bed by Mum around 8 am. She will have laid out breakfast for him and set up the percolator for fresh coffee.

Mum is the only person to come home for lunch and say hello to the dog. (There are more pets in France than in the UK.) Dad has a 90-minute lunch break, the daughter has a sit-down three-course canteen lunch and the son has a snack and a smoke or two on or off the campus, carefully counting the hole that cigarettes are making in his pocket money (*argent de poche*). Cigarette prices have increased by about 50 per cent over the last two years, but are still less than UK prices.

Mum will be home by just after 6 pm unless she pops into the local supermarket for urgent shopping. This supermarket will not necessarily be the cheapest as a discount one, part of the same central buying group, sells some identical products but in different packaging in a no-frills store 5 kms and a few traffic jams away. Dad may have used part of his lunch break to get some DIY material from a shopping centre store. Daughter may have early evening modern dance or ballet classes, followed by a few hours of *baccalauréat* (roughly equivalent to A levels) home-work interspersed with some long mobile phone conversations. There are around 45 million mobiles in France – fewer than in the UK. Son may attend some extra-curricular university activity. Parents dine together around 8 pm, perhaps catching up on world news on TV at the same time.

School activities and children's sports clubs

Interschool sports competitions are not widespread. Their place is largely taken by district sports clubs to which motivated and sometimes non-motivated children coerced by parents, belong from primary school age (six) upwards. An annual subscription which covers insurance, the club's kit and a doctor's fitness certificate gives the right to train and play (the *licence*). Football and basketball clubs (popular with girls) abound. One-day tournaments on a league or knock-out basis are common with younger players who play short matches. Older players (over ten) play home and away matches on a seasonal league basis.

Most swimming pools have sessions exclusively reserved for school pupils as part of their PE lessons. Cinema trips for educative films are also arranged by language or literature teachers. Pupils' parents pay the reduced ticket price, although pupils with extremely poor parents may still be left out.

Schools organise exchange language visits in or out of term time with 'twinned' partner towns in other countries, particularly in Germany and the UK. Away trip nature weeks (*classes vertes*) are also a feature of environmental and scientific education. Skiing weeks (*classes neiges*) are popular. The cost of these week-long *classes* is subsidised so most parents can afford to send their children.

The great escape for pre-adolescent and adolescent children (and for their parents) is summer holiday camps (*colonies*) by the sea, or in the mountains, which last two or three weeks. They are quite independent of school and are usually the first time that parents and children have been separated from each other for any length of time! Summer camps organised by municipalities are reasonably priced.

The importance of the family

It is no surprise that, Christmas aside, Mother's Day (*La Fête des Mères*) on a Sunday at the end of May/early June is the biggest money-spinner in France. Three generations of mothers (great grandmothers, grandmothers and mothers) often celebrate together, not forgetting future mothers among the fourth generation children. Father's Day, by comparison, hardly gets a look in two or three weeks later. Easter, about six weeks earlier, is also an important general family celebration (*fête familiale*), but no longer for religious reasons. It's almost Christmas again for young children with chocolate eggs hidden in the garden for their amusement. The widespread existence of variously sized family *gîtes* ('holiday rental homes in France' is the closest translation) underlines the importance families still give to taking holidays together.

Mothers and daughters have particularly close relationships, the more so the closer you get to the Mediterranean. The family telephone line could well have a hot-line extension for mother-daughter conversations which are, on average, several times a week (sometimes several times a day) on subjects ranging from the day's activities, how long to cook a stew to what's on the box tonight. French families tend to move less than UK families. Careers permitting, several generations of families will spend their lives in the same area, even in the same town. Young grandmothers can become an extension of their daughter's family, picking up her young children from school and baby-sitting regularly. Baby-sitting associations are rare.

Whole TV programmes are devoted to the subject of maternal influence and its positive and negative effects. Celebrities reveal all and psychologists offer their interpretations.

Property inheritance law still mainly benefits descendants and not spouses (see also Chapter 6). Getting wills and testaments right before the time comes can avoid terrible family squabbles. New legislation is proposed for 2007 to ease inheritance problems.

Because of France's pre-eminence in broadband expansion, genealogical research has become popular. Whole family trees, with several branches extending to second cousins three times removed, organise annual lunches, hiring municipal halls or banqueting halls for up to a few hundred people.

Although there is nothing in France to equal the Scottish clan system, identical Corsican family names come close. Any Dominici, Santini, etc will almost certainly claim to be part of the same family. As a regional group Corsicans have an unshakeable sense of identity. A Corsican going into a French Consular office in a third world country where the Consul is Corsican can expect red-carpet treatment.

In North African immigrant families the father may still be trying to lay down his law, respecting former family traditions in his country of origin, which can conflict with the republican laws of France, his adopted country.

Weekends

Reciprocating the lack of an English translation for '*bon appetit!*' the French translation for 'weekend' is a hyphenated '*week-end*'. The British obviously gave the French the idea of taking time off at the end of the working week to particularly enjoy their cooking!

Although the French are not the greatest international travellers (why should they be as France offers sufficient change in scenery (*dépaysement*) to satisfy most people?) they do get about within France at weekends. Lyon is less than two hours by road from skiing in the Savoy Alps and one hour now by train from beaches in Marseille. Paris is less than two hours drive from Normandy beaches. Nice is just over one hour from ski slopes in the southern French Alps. France has several national holidays which are near the end or at the beginning of the week, encouraging an extra day off to bridge an intervening work day (*faire le pont*) and making for a four-day weekend. Coupled with the shorter working week now of 35 hours – four and a half days for millions – the possibilities for long weekends, even abroad now with low-cost flights, are numerous. One out of four executives manage to own a holiday home in France. A 'weekend cottage' interestingly makes some concession to rural France and the French language as it is called a '*maison de campagne*'.

When they are at home at weekends, keeping fit, eating out and doing DIY are popular. Over 50 per cent of the French are homeowners and DIY is a huge business as it is in the UK. It is estimated that one third of the population at any one time have an important home-improvement project (see Chapters 4 and 7). Suburban or area shopping centres are choc-a-bloc. Cinema-going is also big business and attendances have picked up considerably in recent years. The private and public TV channels have an agreement with film distributors not to show films on TV on Saturday evenings. (See Getting the Best out of the Cinema in Chapter 9).

The importance of conversation

French people talk a lot and – it seems to foreigners – quickly. It may be calculated to stop British people getting a word in edgeways and being able to speak on an equal footing with them as *le français* is no longer the international language of diplomacy! Joking apart, there may be several reasons:

1 The *Quid* (French encyclopaedia) states that the French, including Canadian French, language has around half the vocabulary of the British, American and Australian variations of English. This means that it often takes more words in French to express exactly the same meaning in English, which has more precise vocabulary. French descriptions and explanations are extremely logical, but often long-winded.

2 In general the French are more extrovert than the British within their family circle and groups of acquaintances. Even extremely reserved people will give you a detailed opinion on a subject dear to them if you pop them the right question.

3 Sentiments are more readily expressed between and within the sexes, and third party conversations about other people's relationships are, as anywhere, rife. Personal health, and the lack of it, is also another pet topic.

4 In a country where the philosophy exam is obligatory for hundreds of thousands of schoolchildren sitting the *baccalauréat* exam every year, and also headline news on the day it takes place, can one wonder that discussion, reflection and intellectual analysis and conversation are all important in everyday life?

Useful vocabulary

abonnement de travail	season ticket for travel to work
argent de poche	pocket money
baccalauréat	exam, roughly equivalent to A levels
car de ramassage scolaire	school bus
carte d'abonnement	season ticket
carnet (Métro)	book of underground tickets
classes neiges	school skiing trips
classes vertes	school nature trips
co-voiturage	car-sharing
crèche	day nursery

dépaysement	change of scenery
faire le pont	taking off intervening workday for long weekend
fête familiale	family celebration
fonctionnaire	public or civil servant
jardin d'enfants	kindergarten
licence	(sport) membership certificate
lotissement privé	(small or large) private housing estate
lycée	upper secondary school
maison de campagne	weekend cottage
maison familiale	family home
périphérique	inner/outer ringroad
PME/PMI	small/medium-sized businesses/industrial companies
TPE	very small companies

3
The Economy, Politics and Future Developments

The economy

France has a capitalist economy influenced to a considerable extent by the state government which has an interest, sometimes a controlling one, in some of the major industries and services. It is consistently a few places ahead of the UK near the top of the world rankings for gross national product (*PNB: produit national brut*) and the same is true for its per capita rate of production. Germany is consistently a few places ahead of France in both categories. Germany of course has a work force approximately 25 per cent larger than both France and the UK, which have similar workforce numbers. Real per capita purchasing power should be taken into account to see who's getting the best deal. France is behind the UK in this respect, but money isn't everything. *Vive la différence* in the way both countries live! Statistics do show, however, that over the last 30 years the French have seen their real purchasing power just about doubled.

In terms of economic growth – the economy's increased capacity to produce goods and services which makes increased living standards possible – France is still behind the UK and was in the lower half of the European Community table in 2003, before the inclusion of ten new EC member countries in May 2004. In the last decade of the twentieth century France averaged an annual economic growth rate of 1.3 per cent, the UK 1.8 per cent and Germany, which was absorbing the negative economic consequences of its reunification, made no progress at all. The growth rate in France for 2004, however, was approximately 2.5 per cent – ahead of expectations – after almost zero growth in 2003.

Jacques Marseille, who lectures at the Sorbonne university and is head of the *Institut d'Histoire Économique et Sociale*, states in an interview published in the April 2004 issue of *Capital* that France's service companies are the second most important group of exporters in the world. The Carrefour hypermarkets, to take one example, were opening about one store a month in China in 2004. Good news for the future of France as the manufacturing sector of the economy of all developed countries continues to decline.

A summary of the main sectors of the French economy follows.

Agriculture

France has the largest agricultural production in Western Europe and, along with Germany, approximately 35 per cent of its land is cultivated. About five per cent of the national workforce in France still works on the land, which is just over twice the UK rate with around 30 per cent of the UK under cultivation.

Just over 50 per cent of France's agricultural output's value derives from all categories of livestock and fowl farming, and cereals, wheat and wood are also important. There is no long-term tendency to growth and annual production figures in the 1990s showed an overall slight decline in most categories with just wood and pork production holding their own. Vineyard production, which is slightly less than Italy's output, plunged some 16 per cent!

Energy

Natural gas and coal production are now almost non-existent, and the last operating coal mines closed in 2005. Nuclear produced electricity is, however, big business and a huge export earner.

Manufacturing industries

Altogether manufacturing industries employ just over 25 per cent of the workforce (around 22 per cent in the UK). Production of machines and transport vehicles, including the highly successful *TGV* train, is an extremely important sector as is manufactured food. Interestingly, the economic value of manufactured food in the UK is similar to France's. The difference is in what is produced.

Service industries

As in all developed countries service industries are increasingly important. Just under 70 per cent of France's workforce is employed in this sector with slightly over 70 per cent in the UK.

France is the most popular tourist country in the world and tourists from the British Isles (15 million) are just ahead of the Germans (14 million) as the leading group, with the Chinese set to become the leading group over the next ten years. Over 70 million people visit France every year: far ahead of visitors to its neighbouring countries of Spain (52 million tourists) and Italy (40 million tourists) and tourism produces seven per cent of the gross national product. To put these figures into perspective Morocco, a popular tourist country the other side of the Mediterranean, receives just three million tourists annually.

Politics

...it has been said that democracy is the worst form of government except all those other forms that have been tried from time to time... Winston Churchill, 1947

France's electoral system encourages at least double figures in the number of different candidates for elections:

* *cantonales,* for the election of *conseillers généraux* (county councillors) every six years;

* *législatives* (parliamentary) every five years for the *Assemblée Nationale*;

* *municipales* (town hall) every six years;

* *Présidentielle* (Presidential/head of state) now every five years,

* and *régionales* (every six years for the 23 administrative regions).

At first glance this can lead to confusion for the uninformed or misinformed.

The Presidential system

The President is extremely active in representing France abroad and is supreme on defence matters. He also lays down the broad political, social, financial and economic lines he would like the Prime Minister and the government which he (the President) has appointed to follow and in theory lets them get on with the job. In practice, if he is not happy with the government's performance he can replace the Prime Minister and/or direct *Monsieur* or *Madame, le Premier Ministre* to reshuffle the cabinet. There was a major cabinet reshuffle in March 2004 when the Socialist Party had a land-slide victory in the *elections régionales* indicating that the country was highly dissatisfied with the government's performance since its election in April 2002. France's *'non'* in May 2005 to the proposed European constitution led to another cabinet reshuffle and a new Prime Minister.

With the exception of European Parliamentary elections, which are subject to the EC single-ballot rule, all French elections have been subject, since 1988, to first-ballot attainment of more than 50 per cent of valid votes for election of a candidate. With so many different parties this usually means a second ballot in each voting district (*circonscription*) and the non-radical left or right wing candidates often ask electors to vote for the first-ballot left or right-wing leading contender to ensure a comfortable majority. Political parties range from at least two extreme left-wing parties, a nature conservation party advocating hunting, fishing and shooting, the environmentalist Greens, the sagging Communist party and the mainstream Socialist party, to an extremely liberal economy right-wing party, a more central right-wing party (the *UDF*), the current party in government – the conservative *UMP* – and the extreme right-wing *Front National*. Signatures of approval are required from at least 500 mayors to be a candidate in the presidential elections. Not as daunting as it sounds, as there are over 36,000 mayors in France and 'approval' doesn't equal a 'vote'.

Presidential mandates were reduced, in 2000, from every seven to five years in line with Parliamentary elections and this rule will be applied for the first time in 2007. Over the last 20 years there have been several periods of Presidents and opposing political tendency governments 'cohabiting': hardly ideal for coherent political programmes. French voters are as fickle as any other voters and two years are quite sufficient for changes of opinion. The *Front National* caused a major scare in the Presidential elections in 2002 when they trounced the Socialist government voters in the first ballot, coming in second, behind the voters for the out-going right-wing *Président* Chirac. The great majority of left-wing voters of all shades were obliged, using their better judgement but with heavy hearts, to give Jacques Chirac his second Presidential mandate: he was elected with over 80 per cent of the second ballot votes.

Politics and personalities

Politics has an important place throughout the year on French TV channels.

Apart from equal free time during official two week pre-election campaign periods, all channels have regular political programmes where several opposing party leading lights debate noisily (despite the TV chairman's attempt to control the conversation) a theme or defend their party's position or actions. These are not to be confused with interview programmes where the interviewer obtains more orderly information or answers from one key politician. Alain Duhamel, in the Jeremy Paxman mould, is an accomplished and pertinent interviewer.

Politics is also a popular topic of conversation, but best avoided if you encounter someone who has extreme, dogmatic thinking. The voting office and polling booth (*isoloir*) are, by contrast, sacred. No audible opinions are the order of the day immediately before, during and after voting. The only time in recent years that it was politically correct to divulge your voting intentions was just before the April 2002 Presidential election.

The Socialist Party has gained ground since the Presidential elections in 2002 without having a charismatic leader. The *UMP* party's star is undoubtedly their new president, Nicolas Sarkozy, who was previously Minister of the Interior before becoming Finance Minister. Just 50, dynamic, effective and convincing, he has undisguised ambitions to become France's next President in 2007.

The 1990s saw a spate of political intrigues and dubious '*affaires*'. Pierre Bérégovoy committed suicide in April 1993 when he was Prime Minister and a convincing explanation has never been given. An MP (*député*) was shot dead in the Var *département* in 1994 which prompted the Prime Minister Edouard Balladur to call for a thorough investigation into any politicians' dealings in commerce, industry, property and finance which looked in the least suspicious. Two government ministers were imprisoned in that period. Since 1995 private companies have been forbidden to finance political parties or campaigns.

Future developments

Retirement

French people are living longer and longer. They are the European champions of longevity along with the Bulgarians (all that yoghurt) and the Crete islanders (all that fish and olive oil). French workers' social security contributions pay state pensions for the retired.

As so many post-Second World War 'baby boom' people are now arriving at retirement age a major reform to the pension system was long overdue to finance the increasing demand. The new pension regulations law was voted in, after much public shouting and trade union demonstration, in July 2003. One significant change was that public and civil servants now have to work more years, bringing them into line with private companies' employees, in order to inject more social security contributions into the state pension fund. For full details, ask for the *'Ma retraite' mode d'emploi* (Nov. 2003) booklet at your local *Caisse Régionale d'Assurance Maladie* office.

Health

The excellent health service (probably the best in the world) has for years been increasingly less viable and a major review of medical cover and the medicine reimbursement system was necessary. See Living Healthily (page 70) for the principal points in the government's three-year plan to get the cost of running the health service back into the black by 2007.

Following the exceptional heat-wave (*canicule*) in the summer of 2003, with temperatures the hottest in France since 1953, the government issued a Heat-wave Precautions Plan on 31 May 2004. A decision had previously been taken to install air-conditioning in at least one lounge or common-room of all old people's homes by July 2004. An estimated 15,000 people (mostly elderly) died in 2003 as a direct result of the heat-wave, and the government was heavily criticised for not having anticipated a potential catastrophe and organised contingency measures. A new Health Minister was appointed in April 2004. Funding for the government subsidies for these air-conditioning installations and other heat-wave care-for-the-elderly plans is to come from the money saved by doing away with the official Whit Monday holiday which became effective in 2005.

As part of the review of the Health Service three enquiries (one Parliamentary and two professional) were commissioned. Their findings provided the basis for the Health Ministry's Hospital Plan 2007 which sets out proposals for improving hospital administration and increasing investment in the 1,600 public and private hospitals in France between now and 2007.

Defence

Following in the tradition of Concorde aeroplane production there are firm plans for Anglo-French joint production of two or three next-generation aircraft carriers similar to the French flag-ship *Charles de Gaulle*. Unlike the *Charles de Gaulle* they will not be nuclear-powered, but there will be numerous identical components to make economies of scale in production attractive. The main difference in design will be the landing/taking-off strips: 'horizontal' take-off strips for France and 'vertical' take-off strips for the British.

Energy

After some negotiations with the trade unions and a few isolated strike actions the Finance Minister Nicolas Sarkozy, appointed with the 2004 cabinet reshuffle, obtained approval almost on schedule for the Parliamentary vote on the partial privatisation of the national electricity board (EDF). (EDF, incidentally, supply around five million homes in the UK through their London company.) This has opened electricity supply to businesses from other suppliers. From 2007 the domestic users' market will also be open to other suppliers. There are a few outcrops of pollution-free renewable energy wind farms (*éoliennes*), which are not as yet the controversial issue they are in the UK.

Transport

The high-speed *TGV* train, one of the marvels of French technological expertise, operates on almost 20 per cent of France's SNCF 32,000 kilometre national rail network on a mixture of special high-speed track and normal track. Rail travel is healthy. The SNCF claims it accounts for only one per cent of transport generated pollution in France. Tramways are also being created or reintroduced into traffic congested cities as relatively pollution-free means of transport. Bordeaux inaugurated its tramway in early 2004 and both Nice and Toulon have tramway projects.

A major extension to the TGV network will be the construction by 2015 of the Lyon to Turin (Italy) link, making Paris to Turin via Lyon a trip taking just over four hours. Work finally started at the end of 2004 on the *TGV* link between France and Spain and is due for completion in 2009. The rail journey between Perpignan and Barcelona will then take just 50 minutes, instead of the current three hours.

There are also plans to increase by ten per cent the 1,000 passenger capacity of the double-decker 400 metre long *TGV*s running to the Mediterranean, by replacing the engines in the middle of the train with high-performance motorised bogey wheels.

Property

The boom in property prices over the five years up to 2004, which can be likened to the escalation in property prices in the UK in the early 1970s, has now levelled off. People buying at the end of the 1990s have, in some areas, almost doubled their money, creating a whole new world of unwitting property speculators. For first-time buyers, or those with limited capital for home purchase, now is an excellent time to buy a property (see next chapter).

Telecommunications

France Télécom has the monopoly on phone installations using their network of cables. There is, from a customer's view-point, attractive competition between them and other telephone companies such as *Cégétel* and *Télé 2* for phone call business, and they have ambitious plans (see their website www.francetelecom.fr) to operate a range of internet activated services for the home in their 2010 Home Plan (*La maison demain 2010*). France is slightly behind the UK in numbers of households possessing internet.

Useful vocabulary

canicule	heat-wave
circonscription	voting district
croissance	growth
Député	Member of Parliament
EDF: Electricité de France	national electricity company
éolienne	windmill tower
GDF: Gaz de France	national gas company

isoloir	polling booth
PNB: produit national brut	gross national product
retraite	retirement
SNCF: Société Nationale des Chemins de Fer	national railway company

4
Buying a Property

The good news for potential buyers is that property prices have now levelled out and property is still cheaper than in the UK. The mechanics of buying, which may appear complex, are designed to give you the buyer the best possible cover. Gazumping is rare as the initial contract penalises the seller if they change their mind about selling to you.

The cost of buying is, however, more than in the UK; up to 15 per cent of the net purchase price when agent's commission, notary fees (their emoluments, taxes, duty and registration fees), specialist surveys for example with period (*époque, style*) houses, plus possibly an architect's fee, are totalled. The cost of buying a property which is under 5 years old, classed as *neuf* (new) will be less than that of buying a property over 5 years old (*ancien*) as the 'new' property is not subject to local taxes which on *ancien* properties are paid through the notary. Look out for *FNR: Frais de Notaires Réduits* in property advertisements.

With good Gallic logic the size of the property is often expressed in terms of its interior floor surface area excluding garages or workshops/boiler rooms, and planked loft areas with ceilings under 1.80 m high. This net living floor area is the *surface habitable (SH)*. The *SH* is particularly useful for immediate appraisal as to whether accommodation is poky, normal or spacious: 25 m^2 is a fair size for a combined lounge and dining room, 10 m^2 is a good-sized kitchen, 8 m^2 a small bedroom and 12 m^2 a fair-sized bedroom. 100 m^2 *SH* is therefore a normal size for a three-bedroomed house and tending towards spacious for a bungalow.

Visiting and negotiating

If you have not yet decided where you plan to buy and the type of property you envisage, considerable initial 'prospecting' can be accomplished from your UK home by studying the property pages and advertisements in the quality Sunday papers and subscribing to English-language French property magazines. A brief survey of types of property and price comparisons throughout France is given at the end of this chapter and various property search websites (in French, or English and French) are listed and described under Useful Websites at the end of this book.

Any property owner will know that location, location and yet again location are the three all-important considerations when buying a property! Add to these, property aspect if you're buying a property in a sunny area (the area roughly below an imaginary line between Bordeaux, Valence and Briançon in the Southern French Alps). Living rooms facing south-east, south or south-west, or all three, are important if you want morning, midday, afternoon or all-day sun, provided, of course, you don't have a mountain towering in front of your home. Forest localities particularly, in the Provence *départements*, Bouches du Rhône and Var, are fire-risk areas (*zones à risque*) in summer. Although new or further planning permission may no longer be granted, this does not of course preclude sales of existing properties.

Finding a property

A subscription to *French Property News*, published monthly by French Property News, 6 Burgess Mews, Wimbledon, London SW19 1UF and/or *Focus on France*, published every two months by Outbound Publishing, 1 Commercial Road, Eastbourne, East Sussex BN21 3XQ are worthwhile. Each of these magazines has lively, informative property articles and carries colour advertisements and both organise major French property shows in the UK.

In many areas of France there will be free copies of the two leading French property colour advertisement magazines, *MagImmo* and *Logic-Immo*, on display in front of estate agents (*agences immobilières*), bakers (*boulangeries*), petrol stations (*stations d'essence*) etc.

Getting professional help

Although over 50 per cent of property sales in France are negotiated directly between seller and buyer, the great majority of these transactions are between French people who at least understand the content, but not necessarily the implications, of the wording in property documents. The final deed of sale contract (*acte authentique*) must be drawn up by a notary who is usually appointed by the seller. *You are strongly advised, especially if you are purchasing for the first time in France, to seek a property through an estate agent or notary, or at least be accompanied by a bilingual, qualified 'search agent' whom you have appointed to act in your interests.* In Britanny, where almost 80 per cent of foreign buyers are British, most estate agents in the popular inland areas have a member of staff who speaks English well.

Both estate agents and notaries should have an official brief (*mandat de vente*) from the property owner indicating that they (estate agent or notary) have been retained to promote and negotiate the sale of the property. The mandate must have the signatures of all the property's owners – especially important in divorce cases – to avoid wasting everybody's time if the property cannot actually be put up for sale.

Exclusive mandates are rare, which is why the potential buyer will often be asked to sign a slip (*bon de visite*), sometimes before the visit, which briefly describes the property visited, date visited, the precise address and the property's asking price which includes the negotiation fee or commission. As properties are not always offered to agents at the same price by owners, or a reduction in price is not communicated to all agents concerned, the *bon de visite* quite logically precludes any double or direct dealing with the seller or another 'cheaper' agent. Estate agents' commission is on a sliding percentage scale with higher priced properties attracting lower rates. These percentages should be prominently displayed in the estate agents' office. Notaries have standard sliding scale negotiating fees throughout France.

Estate agents will normally ferry foreign buyers around to properties even if they (the agents) do have the keys and an exclusive mandate. They will naturally be keen to book foreign visitors for as much of their time as possible once the visitor's property requirements and seriousness have been established. A visitor with a full programme of visits will have less time to visit through a competitor. Properties which obviously do not fit the bill may be shown to accentuate the advantages of a more attractive property. Traditionally, property information details have been skimpy in estate agents, but with the arrival of virtual reality computer images and computer-linked pools of data through estate agency chains such as *Orpi, Century 21, La Forêt* and *ERA*, a lot of time-wasting visits can now be avoided.

Knowing what you're buying

Property advertisements the world over eulogise and computer-generated images often look better than the real thing, so if and when the actual property does bowl you over, the '*coup de coeur*', be rational and don't forget to ask the following questions or check the following points (the list is not exhaustive).

Planning permission

Are extensions and/or improvements possible if you have this in mind? Check the local regulations at the *service d'urbanisme* at the town hall. The planning permission density for the plot on which the property is built may be up to its limit. The *COS* (*coefficient d'occupation des sols*) which determines this may be, for example, 0.20 (or 20 per cent). If the property already occupies 200 m^2 ground area on an overall plot of 1,000 m^2 this means that no further building will be permitted unless the regulations are revised at some future date. Don't confuse *COS* with *SHON* (*surface hors oeuvre nette*). The *SHON* is the total of all interior habitable floor areas. A bungalow occupying the same ground area as a two-floor house will obviously have a smaller *SHON*.

Bear in mind that any extension or new building project application which will take the total *surface habitable* to over 170 m^2 must be accompanied by an architect's plans.

Plot size

Is the accurate plot size given? Detached properties with large gardens which are not part of a private housing estate (*lotissement privé*) often have approximate plot sizes (*terrain d'environ XX m^2*). The land registry department (*service de cadastre*) at the town hall will give you the official figure and the precise boundaries of the land.

Housing estates

Private housing estates will normally have an *association de co-propriétaires* (property owners' association) which manages the common-owned areas (private access road(s), pavements, trees, outside gardens, parking areas, access gate, etc) and convenes annually to deliver the accounts for the reserve maintenance funds and vote on decisions for future repairs and improvements. Ask to see the annual reports and accounts.

Flats

Flats are nearly always sold freehold. Maintenance charges for blocks of flats, especially de luxe ones (*résidences de standing*) with beautifully laid-out and maintained private gardens, communal swimming pool and tennis court, underground parking, lifts and caretaker/concierge are an important consideration. Ask the sales agent or the managing agents (*le syndic*) who manage the block on behalf of the individual owners (*co-propriétaires*) to give you a copy of the *réglementation de la co-propriété* and also details of any improvement or renovation work which has been voted for.

The *Réglementation* will confirm the reference number (*lot numéro*) of the flat in which you are interested and the *surface habitable* will also be certified under the Carrez Law regulations, so no mistake can be made as to exactly which flat will appear on the sales contracts. Under the Carrez Law dimensions must be correct to within five per cent. Incorrect measurements (ie a smaller area) subsequently certified by a surveyor are grounds for renegotiating the sale price proportionally. (The Carrez Law also applies to habitable areas for houses in private housing estates.)

If the work voted for has not been invoiced before the final act of sale is signed, you, as the new owner, will have to foot the flat's part of the bill.

Façade face-lifts and lift maintenance charges are two particularly important costs. Face-lift (*ravalement*) costs and most other costs which affect the general maintenance of the building are calculated on a pro-rata basis taking into account individual flats' *surface habitable*, storey and outlook and whether they have a cellar/parking space/garage. Lift maintenance charges should be lowest for first floor flats and highest for the top floor. A nicely-finished flat in a two or three-floor *résidence* with a sea-view and 150 metres from a swimming beach on the Mediterranean, away from the top-end area of the market (the Côte d'Azur) can have surprisingly low maintenance charges if there is no lift, no swimming pool and the flat has its own heating. They exist.

If the heating is a central system for a block of flats you will be invoiced pro-rata according to the size of the flat and, from 2006, all flats must have individual water meters.

Finding information

Sellers or their agents for houses and flats are obliged, in the following instances, to inform you about the presence (or absence) of asbestos in construction materials, lead-content paints, and termites:

Asbestos

Asbestos (*amiante*) has been an illegal building material since the end of 1996. If the property was built before 1 July 1997 the seller must certify its presence or absence. If it is present (false ceilings are often guilty) and the certificate indicates that it is expelling dust with more than five fibres of asbestos per litre of air, the owner now has to cover it completely and effectively, or have it removed. At the moment this regulation does not apply to non-residential areas such as staircases and cellars in flat blocks. This is due to change at the end of 2005.

Lead-content paint

Lead-content paint (*peinture au plomb*) has been illegal in buildings since 1948. Pre-1948 buildings must produce a certificate indicating presence or absence. If the original lead-content layer of paint has been painted or wall-papered over it is considered to be 'inaccessible' and thus not dangerous. If, however, it is judged officially by local authorities to be 'accessible' the seller must have it stripped off before selling the property.

Termites

Is the property in one of the 3,000 municipalities in over half of France's *départements* officially declared a termite-risk area? Consult www.termite.com.fr for areas concerned and information (in French) on the problem generally. A proprietor selling their home in these 'official' areas should produce a certificate confirming presence or absence of termites. If the seller is not prepared to have a specialist company treat the problem it may be sound judgement to withdraw from negotiations. Beware of areas not classified officially as infested areas, but which are next to official risk-areas.

Most of the above information should be provided without having to ask. There may though be other things you want to check out yourself, such as if it's a windy spot, if there are noisy schoolchildren from the local school in term-time or if there's a lot of tourist traffic in the school holiday period.

Ask in particular also for the land tax (*taxe fonçière*) amount which is payable annually to the local community. This may vary considerably between adjacent municipalities.

Depending on the state of the market it is reasonable to make an offer within five per cent of the asking price. 'Divorce case' (*divorce*) properties may be advertised at slightly lower 'divorce' prices to encourage a quick sale provided the divorcing couple agree!

Useful vocabulary

acte authentique	deed of sale
amiante	asbestos
bon de visite	certificate confirming visit
coefficient d'occupation des sols	planning density
co-propriétaire	house or flat owner in block or estate
coup de cœur	completely captivated
lotissement privé	private property estate
maison ancien	over 5 years old house classification, or description of old-style house
maison neuf	under 5 years old house classification
maison d'époque	period house
maison, style...	house from the...period or in the ...style
mandat de vente	sales mandate
peinture au plomb	lead-content paint
ravalement	face-lift
standing	luxury, de-luxe
surface hors œuvre nette	total interior habitable floor area excluding machine/boiler rooms etc
syndic	estate or block's managing agent
Service de Cadastre	Land Registry
Service d'Urbanisme	Town Planning Department
taxe fonçière	land tax
taxe d'habitation	community tax
terrain	plot
zone à risque	risk area

The Buying Procedure

Two preliminary sales contracts are possible after the verbal or written offer (*offre d'achat*) has been accepted:

- the *compromis de vente*

- or the *promesse unilatérale de vente*.

Both contracts specify the precise address of the property and its total habitable space with a brief description (number of rooms and their functions), the agreed price and the agent's commission (normally included in the sales price), completion and possession dates (usually a three-month period). It is important at this point to detail fixtures, fittings and equipment such as fitted bathrooms and kitchens which will remain part of the property.

Both contracts ask for immediate deposits, held in a sequestered account, of up to ten per cent of the purchase price.

The *unilatérale* contract

The *unilatérale* contract does not commit the buyer to purchase the property whereas the seller is bound to reserve the property for the potential buyer at an agreed price for an agreed period of time. Deferment clauses (*conditions suspensives*) should be included in both contracts making the purchase subject to any required finance being obtained – it is advisable to detail the nature of the loan and the organisation concerned – and null and void if a local town planning decision is revealed which will depreciate the value of the property. The buyer's deposit is returned in these instances. A *droit de préemption* clause will also ensure that, in the event of a compulsory purchase order before completion which precludes the sale, the buyer recovers their deposit.

The *compromis* contract

The *compromis* is the contract more frequently used. Estate agents are quite accustomed to drawing up these preliminary contracts. If you are dealing directly with a seller you are advised to have the preliminary contract drawn up and signed before a notary, preferably the one who will draw up the *acte authentique*. Bilingual assistance from a qualified person is also strongly recommended when signing agreement to documents as they will usually only be in French.

Useful information

- A seven-day cooling-off period was introduced a few years ago giving the buyer additional protection at this stage. Buyers can change their minds, no questions asked, within seven days of signing a preliminary contract.

- During the three-month period prior to the *acte de vente definitive/acte authentique* the *notaire* verifies property title, outstanding loans, charges, obtains the asbestos, termite and lead-free paint certificates (if they have not already been produced) and checks land registry details and town planning regulations.

- The completion deed reconfirms the information given in the preliminary contract, with more detailed information on the house or flat, outbuildings and land, and with the exclusion of any previous suspensive clauses.

- Estimated notary fees, which are of course in addition to any negotiating fees if the notary also acts as the sales agents, are given under *'frais de notaires'* in the notaries' website www.immonot.com.

Useful vocabulary	
compromis de vente	preliminary sales contract
conditions suspensives	deferment conditions
droit de préemption	pre-emptive right
offre d'achat	formal purchase offer
promesse unilatérale de vente	unilateral preliminary sales contract

Property types and prices

Appartement dans immeuble. Flat in block, perhaps in urban area without private grounds.

Appartement dans résidence. Flat in block of flats, normally with private grounds.

Appartement dans villa. Flat conversion in old or new house, with or without garden. Low maintenance charges, if any.

Architect-planned villas (*villa d'architecte*). All houses built since 1979 exceeding 170 m² living space are architect-designed. Often with large, open-plan living areas and kitchens and if, in addition, initially owned by an architect, particularly well built. Size means they are often detached (*individuelle*) on plots over 1,000 m² and not in private estates with small plots. Style respects regional regulations.

Bastide. Substantial, stone-built, traditional Mediterranean house, usually in an inland village or rural situation. May feature outside open-stone work (*pierres apparentes*).

Chalets. The most prestigious alpine ski-resorts have new and recent chalets of all sizes, some of which are immaculate replicas, with wood throughout, of authentic old gems.

Château. Renaissance, or later, stately house, best translated as 'château'!

Château féodal/château fort. Castle (mainly medieval), which sometimes comes with water-filled moats (*douves en eau*).

Chaumières. Thatched houses, cottages, *fermettes* (small farmhouses).

Duplex. Self-contained two-floor flat in block or, like a maisonette, in a larger house or building.

Gentilhommière. Small manor (*manoir*). Should have its own grounds (*parc*).

Hôtel particulier. A period town mansion with several floors and usually garret rooms (*chambres de bonne*).

Loft. Not a low-ceilinged attic conversion. The *loft*, a 1990s creation, is a spacious, open, high-ceilinged, contemporary, top floor or sometimes top two floors *appartement* or former office conversion.

Longère. Long-roofed traditional property predominant in Britanny. Period *longères* have hand-cut slate tile roofs, sometimes with dormer windows, and are granite built.

Mas. Provençal farmhouse or farmhouse buildings with rustic kitchen and perhaps traditional exposed beam (*poutres apparentes*) ceilings.

Maison à colombage. Half-timbered character properties. A Normandy speciality but not exclusive to that region.

Maison de maître. Large old country house or large *bourgeois* style town house (possibly with garret rooms), with elegant interior decorative features.

Maison de village. An old village house, usually terraced or semi-detached (*mitoyenne*), with at least ground and upper floor.

Pavillon. A small house with a garden or old lodges in country estates.

Villa club. Small house designed as a holiday home.

Speciality properties

Speciality properties include converted farm and rural buildings such as *bergeries* (stone-built sheep shelters), *colombiers* (dovecotes), *granges* (barns), *maisons de chasse* (hunting lodges), *moulins* (mills) and *pressoirs* (press-houses). There are also converted *monastères* (monasteries) and *couvents* (convents). Chapels usually remain *chapelles*.

Vineyard properties (*propriétés viticoles*) vary in size tremendously so price comparisons are difficult. Vineyards in the Burgundy region do, however, command higher prices generally than those in the South-West area which includes Bordeaux.

Property areas

The most expensive property areas are the city of Paris and the Paris area (Ile de France), the Côte d'Azur, particularly the Cannes-Antibes area, and certain prestigious ski resorts in the Savoy Alps. Town centre properties cost more than rural properties and properties on any of the three coastlines in France, particularly those with sea-views, always have a higher market price than those just a few kilometres inland. Major cities such as Montpellier, which continues to develop at a great pace, Strasbourg, the seat of the European Parliament, and Marseille, now rapidly reached with the *TGV* train, have seen dramatic price increases in the last few years.

Below is a survey giving average property transaction prices, supplied by the French notaries' website www.immoprix.com, for the last available 12 month period for towns and areas throughout France likely to be of most interest to UK purchasers.

Paris	16th *arrondissement*. Bois de Boulogne area. 5,000€ per m^2. *Ancien* (over 5 years old) properties
Paris	6th *arrondissement*. Heart of the Left Bank area. 6,440€ per m^2. *Ancien* properties
Ile-de-France	Val-d'Oise *département*. 1,649€ per m^2. Apartments
Ile-de-France	Seine-St-Denis *département*. 1,708€ per m^2. Apartments
Strasbourg	1,642€ per m^2. *Ancien* apartments 1,879€ per m^2. New apartments

Areas	Houses (*anciens*) €	Apartments (*anciens*) €/m^2	Apartments (*neufs*) €/m^2
Aquitaine			
Agen	124,115	1,092	1,872
Bergerac	117,975	not given	not given
Bordeaux	203,666	1,636	1,851
Talence	178,202	1,445	2,082
Mont-de-Marsan	133,212	1,317	1,644
Britanny			
Dinan	139,809	1,638	not given
Châteauneuf-du-Faou	79,439	not given	not given
Fougères	117,636	916	not given
Combourg, Callac and Huelgoat also attract British buyers seeking old houses			
Burgundy			
Dijon	198,493	1,534	1,789
Centre/Pays de la Loire			
Blois	144,137	1,220	1,814
Nantes	218,507	1,811	2,187
Orléans	160,701	1,422	1,769
Tours	150,946	1,392	1,725

Languedoc-Roussillon			
Agde	159,455	2,070	1,921
Béziers	141,044	1,030	1,916
Montpellier	228,130	1,953	2,269
Nîmes	163,519	1,562	1,960
Limousin			
Haute-Vienne	105,727	1,087	1,166
Corrèze	101,270	1,166	not given
Creuse	62,453	not given	1,622
Midi-Pyrénées			
Albi	142,430	1,293	1,759
Toulouse	231,719	1,683	1,992
Normandy			
Caen	149,014	1,508	1,836
Pas-de-Calais			
Arras	111,370	1,375	1,601
Provence/Alpes de Haute Provence/Côte d'Azur			
Aix-en-Provence	435,700	2,642	3,380
Alpes de Haute Provence	138,528	1,218	2,319
Avignon	182,896	1,274	2,187
Antibes	375,490	2,713	3,504
Draguignan area	429,994	2,673	2,853
Grasse	434,361	3,003	3,030
Hyères	299,846	2,632	2,733
Nice	324,149	2,529	2,843
St-Raphaël	466,274	2,914	3,413
Savoy Alps			
Chambéry	234,061	1,656	1,912
Chamonix-Mont Blanc	not given	4,173	5,053
Evian-les-Bains	not given	2,066	2,153
Valloire	not given	2,394	3,208

Different ways of buying

Buying on plan

The principal advantages of buying a house or flat on plan are that the price is fixed from the outset and the construction materials and design have already been chosen by the developer or construction company's architect so the buyer has no need to worry about appointing an architect.

Many flat developers also have several interior equipment options at pre-fixed prices and sometimes room layouts can be modified at the blue-print stage, ie before building commences. With housing estates there will be a choice of property designs, finishes and sizes although you may not be able to build the particular property you like most on the plot you like most. Watch out for planning restrictions. Houses may sometimes have to be built in a joined block of three with the two outside houses semi-detached and the middle one, terraced, on what may be the nicest plot.

With both flat developments and housing estates, the location has been found by the developer. If you are having a house built which is not part of a housing development programme you may have to find the plot yourself, checking through the town hall that it can be built on (*terrain constructible*) and ascertaining any particular building limitations.

In all instances it is prudent to consult the local urbanisation plan (*plan local d'urbanisme: PLU*) at the *service d'urbanisme* at the town hall. These plans are revised about once a decade. Find out when it was last revised. Can another block of flats be built between you and the sea if you're in a low-level block? Will your country view remain completely unrestricted (*imprenable*)? Have discussions about a possible nearby motorway been going on for years? An 'N' on town planning areas indicates green belts.

Before signing the reservation contract (*contrat de reservation*) for a flat ask the developer to show you on the *Réglementation de la Co-propriété* what type of shops (if any), restaurants, small businesses etc are planned in your block. Are there likely to be any noisy or smelly ones? Check that the developer or house builder has financial liability insurance to cover you if they go bankrupt before finishing the construction: a *garantie d'achèvement bancaire*. For house builders, it is advisable to deal with a member of the national house-builders association (*UNCMI: Union*

Nationale des Constructeurs de Maisons Individuelles).

Details of the construction materials and utilities provided should be confirmed in the technical details prospectus. The type of heating (gas is preferable and is a good re-sale feature), sound-proofing materials used (especially important in flats) and type of taps used (will they last?) are all important.

Once your preliminary enquiries, including a visit to any identical show-houses or flats *(appartements/maisons témoins)*, have been completed to your satisfaction, five per cent of the sale price is deposited upon signature of the reservation contract. The definite sales contract *(contrat de vente en l'état future d'achèvement)* may, in the case of flats, be signed much later on as the developer has to ensure enough flats have been sold to make the project viable before starting any work. A two per cent deposit may only be required if the definite sales contract is likely to be signed one year after the reservation contract. Deposits are returned if the development does not get off the ground!

Demands for stage payments, laid down by law for on-plan constructions and which should be accompanied by an architect's certificate indicating the stage to which work has been done (essential if you're not on the spot), are as follows:

• five per cent (or two per cent, see above) on reservation;

• 35 per cent on completion of the foundations;

• 70 per cent when the roof is finished *(hors d'eau)*;

• 95 per cent when construction inside and outside is completed;

• the final five per cent in exchange for the property keys following your final tour of inspection.

Buying a building plot

Buying and then blocking a building plot for several years is not possible. Long-term speculation is not the name of the game. A building project must be completed within four years of plot purchase – unless *force majeure* circumstances can be shown – and construction work *started* within two years of obtaining the planning permission *(permis de construire)*.

Most importantly ascertain before deciding to buy, through your notary or directly with the town hall or *Direction Départementale de l'Equipement: DDE*, that the land you like is building land. At the same time check, as with property developments (above), the *PLU* plans.

A notary will be able to trace exact title and any rights-of-way (*droits de servitude*) conditions. Rivers are in the public domain so a lovely navigable river going across extensive grounds can invite complete strangers to paddle across your land. Similarly, private beach land is only private up to 5 metres from the sea. Do you want surfers knocking at your gate?

A surveyor (*géomètre*) can be appointed to determine and mark out the precise limits of individual plots which are not part of estate projects. They can also advise or obtain advice on the construction suitability of the land if it is particularly uneven or rocky. Ask them about the anti-frost depth norms (*profondeurs de garde au gel*) for foundations in the area for one and two-floor homes. Beware of nearby tree-barren hillsides in rainy areas which can become landslides after heavy rain, and flood-risk areas. Properties may have been built in these areas before and the land may not yet be officially classed as a *zone à risqué* and *non-constructible*.

Buying a plot in a private housing development programme means you won't have to worry about having the access road made up and services laid on. Look for '*terrains/parcelles viabilisés*' in advertisements.

Construction guarantees for houses

When you hand over the final five per cent of the stage payments you receive the keys and sign off the work completed report (*procès verbal de réception*). The satisfactorily completed work guarantee (*garantie de parfait achèvement*) runs from that time and gives you one year to indicate any imperfections that were not apparent on completion.

This guarantee is completed by the 10-year construction guarantee (*garantie décenniale*) which covers any defects threatening solidity of the construction or correct functioning of its integral fixtures, such as baths. Defects due to soil subsidence are covered. The two-year guarantee (*garantie biennale de bon fonctionnement*) covers all items and equipments and their proper working order, such as taps, boilers, blinds, doors and electrical equipment which can be removed without damaging the building structurally. Of course, if you've invested wisely in material options, from fitted kitchens to taps and double-glazed windows, the manufacturers' guarantees for the materials themselves will be a lot longer.

These guarantees also apply to extension constructions and improvements to existing properties if you're renovating.

Property auctions

If you're not in a hurry, but able to produce funds quickly when necessary, wait and watch newspaper advertisements and official announcements for *appartements/ maisons/propriétés vendues aux enchères.* The reserve price fixed by the notary for *vente par adjudication* sales can be 35 per cent less than the market evaluation.

A viewing date is set before the actual auction. If you confirm interest, a certified cheque (returnable) for up to 20 per cent of the reserve price (*mise à prix*) must be deposited with the auctioneers so that you can officially participate. The exact percentage depends on whether the auction is a *vente judicaire* with bids through the tribunal's *avocat* (barrister) and the creditor fixing the reserve price or a *vente par adjudication devant notaire* (before a notary) when the notary, as mentioned above, fixes the reserve price.

Tenders

If you're interested in the stately-home business, properties in the public domain, which may be listed buildings (see below), are sometimes offered for sale by tender with sealed bids sent to the appointed notary.

Buying for renovation

Your heart may be set on a period property or a particular location where the existing property requires modernisation and/or an extension for your accommodation requirements.

The precise dates of period properties are difficult to certify with complete accuracy as notaries only trace ownership back over the last 30 years or so. Employ an expert (*expert en immobilier*) to verify at least the period authenticity, check the main drainage (*tout à l'égout*) or septic tank (*fosse septique*) system, foundations, walls, roof and electrical wiring and also to give you their valuation. Thatched roofs should be completely renewed about every 40 years (160 m^2 of roof space can take a month) and checked every one or two years. Are skilled craftsmen who still know how to faithfully restore run-down property to its former glory available locally – and, ideally, original building materials? Ask to see bills (*factures*) for major work completed in recent years in a property which interests you. They should be available for any work that is still covered by a ten-year construction guarantee.

If the property is subject to a preservation order as a listed building (*Monument Historique: MH*) or registered on the more prestigious *Inventaire Supplémentaire des Monuments Historiques: ISMH* list, you will need official approval for any work and in particular modifications proposed. Permits take a notoriously long time to obtain and projects submitted by an architect (even though one may not be strictly necessary) are viewed more favourably. The cost of the work is offset against income tax liability provided part of the property can still be visited by the public. Any work to an *ISMH* property is subject to this condition and a public domain *ISMH* property will usually only be sold if the public can continue to view it.

Costs and regulations

It is important to cost improvements, extensions and renovations correctly, allowing for a generous margin of error, as initial guesstimate budgets inevitably prove to be insufficient. Delays for completion of work should also be stipulated in the written estimates (preferably three) that you obtain. Consider employing an architect to oversee the work if you're not on the spot. The cost of their services can be recouped with the savings they effect and they will also ensure that national and local building regulations are complied with, for non-listed buildings, and that the request for planning permission (*permis de construire*) is deposited with all the right paperwork at the local authority's office. An architect is not recommended if your project only requires you to deposit an official notification of work (*déclaration de travaux*). The town planning regulations applicable throughout France (*Code de l'Urbanisme: CU*), available at the town hall or *DDE* office, sets out building regulations.

Building companies approved by the *Qualibat* organisation bear the distinctive blue and white pyramid logo on their headed letter paper. All building work except electrical is covered. Approved electrical installation companies' letterhead bears the blue-striped QE *Qualifelec* logo. Approval by either of these independent organisations is a mark of technical competence. *Qualibat* approval is also an indication that a company is appropriately registered and has adequate insurance cover and sound financial standing. If you have a little basic French, visit www.qualibat.com and www.qualifelec.fr for area lists of approved companies.

Ideally, use a registered company with the appropriate seal of approval on their letterheading, and whose work you have seen and which has been strongly recommended. Don't confuse a friend of a friend with a serious recommendation. Estate agents can also introduce you to builders. *ORPI*, one of the national estate agency chains, makes this part of their service charter for potential buyers.

VAT (*TVA*) is particularly low at 5.5 per cent – at least until the end of 2005 – on all conversion, improvement, renovation and transformation work carried out by professional builders to any residential property that is over two years old. Materials, with certain exceptions, are also subject to 5.5 per cent VAT provided they are supplied and invoiced by the same company that does the work. Any new construction, extension, verandah or other additional living space (ceiling height over 1.80 m) is subject to the much higher VAT rate of 19.6 per cent. Note that attic conversion is not considered as construction work if the roof outline stays the same.

Useful vocabulary

avocat	barrister
appartements/ maisons témoins	show-flat/house
contrat de vente en l'état de futur achèvement	sales contract for future home completion
déclaration de travaux	official notification of work project
droits de mutation	land transfer tax
droits de servitude	rights of way
facture	invoice
fosse septique	septic tank
garantie biennale de bon fonctionnement	two-year guarantee (non-structural)
garantie décennale	ten-year structural guarantee
garantie de parfait achèvement	satisfactorily-completed work guarantee
hors d'eau	roof-covered
mise à prix	reserve price
permis de construire	planning permission
profondeur de garde au gel	anti-frost depth norms
procès verbal de réception	work completed report

propriété vendue aux enchères	property auction
service d'urbanisme	town planning department
terrain constructible	building land
terrain viabilisé	plot with made-up road/services laid on
tout à l'égout	mains drainage
TVA	VAT

PART TWO

LIVING IN FRANCE

5
Day-to-Day Living

Improving or learning the language

It will help your long-term career, integration or holiday plans if you understand 100 per cent of what is being said and written, even if you yourself never attain absolute perfection in the written or spoken word. An exception is in the enclave of Monaco, where speaking good English, which suggests you've got a healthy bank balance, usually gets you a better reception than speaking passable French.

Although employees of multi-national companies will correspond, converse and prepare official reports, especially technical ones, between their national offices in English, in-house meetings and work will require a certain level of proficiency in French. All companies in France with more than ten members of staff are obliged to invest 1.6 per cent of their annual salary bill in professional training for employees if they don't have an internal company training division. Ideally, for foreign employees, teachers in external French-language teaching companies should be ex-business or technical people who have subsequently qualified as teachers of their language.

Unemployed people registered with the *Agence Nationale Pour l'Emploi: ANPE* (National Employment Agency) may be entitled to partially or completely subsidised French courses if they already have a basic level and can demonstrate that a better level will help to get them employment corresponding to their experience.

Finding a language course

Retirees, or anyone else who wants to improve their French primarily for personal or social reasons, have several possibilities. The *Alliance Française* (similar to the British Council) promotes the French language and culture through written and spoken teaching courses and the organisation of inter-cultural functions, shows and meetings. It has organisations in Antibes, Barr, Bordeaux, Brive-la-Gaillarde, Cap d'Ail, Cherbourg, Clermont-Ferrand, Dieppe, Dijon, Grasse, Grenoble, Les Sables d'Olonne, Le Touquet, Lyon, Marseille, Montpellier, Nice, Paris (head office), Rouen, Saverne, Strasbourg, Thann, Toulouse, Tours, Tulle, Valenciennes, Vendôme, Vichy and Wasselonne. The website www.alliancefr.org has fuller details, in English. Tours, in the Indre-et-Loire *département*, has the reputation of being the 'Oxford' of France because of the neutral, clear accents of its native inhabitants. The UK's Foreign Office has been known to send diplomatic staff there for French lessons. Interestingly, country people known as *'berrichons'* from the Berry area which extends mainly over the two neighbouring *départements* of Cher and Indre have broad accents and heavily rolled r's. Canny Scotsmen who speak good French can pass themselves off as *berrichons*.

If you live or holiday in South-East France, Britanny or Normandy the English website www.angloinfo.com has information on language schools in these areas. The British Embassy (Paris) or the Consulate Office in Amiens, Biarritz, Bordeaux, Boulogne-sur-Mer, Calais, Dinard, Dunkerque, Le Havre, Lille, Lyon, Marseille, Nantes or Nice may also suggest websites to consult for information, although they cannot as a government organisation send out addresses for individual schools or give recommendations. Visit also www.britishembassy.gov.uk/france.

Other ways of learning

Qualified private or state-school teachers often advertise in small ads in shop windows. Classes arranged with these teachers directly on an *ad hoc* basis have advantages and disadvantages. You pay as you learn and stop when you want, and opting out is easy. The going rate is around 23€ per hour, which for individual tuition at your or their home is cheaper than a one-to-one class in language school premises. Students who advertise their teaching services, undercutting qualified teachers' prices, at around 15€ per hour, are not necessarily a good solution. Language school group classes should of course be cheaper than individual language school tuition.

Watching and listening to TV news, including weather forecasts, is good comprehension practice and reading the French sub-titles for English-language films on the *Arte* evening channel helps to speed up your reading rate. Sub-titles are necessarily summaries of dialogue and are not strict translations.

Becoming fluent

You can really start congratulating yourself (don't worry if it never happens) when you calculate arithmetically in French, especially if the results are still right. Remember – and this is essential when writing cheques – that written (and printed/typed) decimal points become commas, 7s should be written with a horizontal line through the stem and dots or spaces should be left between thousands when written/typed as numbers. For example, a British 534,000.52 becomes 534.000,52 or 534 000,52.

However proficient you become, your English accent may stick. You will know if you're stuck with a pronounced accent if, after several years' residence, people begin to congratulate you on your excellent French, implying that you speak very well for a visitor or for someone who has just moved to France. If you want to be remembered in an impersonal business world it is, however, a tremendous plus and can also open many sealed doors (see Chapter 12). Women seem to have more success in losing their accents than men. Notable (deliberate?) exceptions are Petula Clark whose career switched to France over 30 years ago and Jane Birkin, relatively unknown in the UK, whose career took off in France. Charlotte Rampling, who does have a good French accent, looks like a natural successor to Jeanne Moreau, the former *femme fatale* of French cinema.

Tutoiement

Several paragraphs could be written on the fascinating subject of when and when not to use the informal *tu* and *toi* (*tutoiement*) and formal *vous* (*vouvoiement*) second person singular pronouns. It is important to understand the basic principles so that the distinction becomes an automatic reflex in appropriate circumstances. The *Le Robert and Collins Senior Dictionary* says 'There are no hard and fast rules...Small children can be addressed as 'tu'...Among the older generation '*vous*' is standard until people know each other well...'. Additionally, animals should be addressed using *tutoiement*, not that they'll be offended by a *vous*.

If you wish to remain formal initially, perhaps in an office environment until you've made your mark, stick to *vous*, not accepting *tu* lightly. This will earn a certain respect. Using Christian names, now customary in a lot of businesses especially between colleagues with similar levels of responsibilities, does not necessarily open the way for *tu* and *toi*. In family circles it is not unusual for mothers- or fathers-in-law to be addressed *vous* by their daughters- and sons-in-law, with *Madame* or *Monsieur* being much too formal.

When you write formal letters to banks, local administrative offices, etc – and everybody living in France for a period of time will have a few of these to do – do get the formal opening and closing of letters right. See Bureaucracy in Chapter 12 for examples. *Vous* is mandatory.

Integration

Don't expect neighbours to come round with a cup of coffee if you've just moved in and are having the cooker plugged in. Nods of the head and formal *Bonjours!* are par for the course, at least in the early days. Make yourself known to the mayor, particularly if you're in a small village which is already full of foreigners, or conversely where you may be the only foreigner. Either way it is a wise move. He or she is always addressed publicly as *Monsieur* or *Madame le Maire*. You may decide to vote for him or her in the next municipal elections (see EC Nationals' Voting Rights in Chapter 6). If you have an unusual property renovation/business project which requires special consideration it may help to swing the balance in your favour.

The town hall and tourist office (*office de tourisme/syndicat d'initiative*) are mines of information on local associations, clubs and forthcoming events, and the *Service des Sports* normally publishes an annual free guide to local sporting events and sports clubs. Dynamic communities have municipal exhibition centres with a continuous calendar of painting or sculpture *vernissages* (exhibition openings with free cocktails): a pleasant early-evening way to socialise and enjoy art. Get your name on the municipal mailing list so you don't miss out.

In small communities the town hall may occasionally ask you to translate something into English once your proficiency in French is recognised. It may ask you to be an unofficial interpreter if a local commemoration ceremony, such as the recent sixtieth anniversaries of the D-Day landings in Normandy and the Allied landings in

Provence, involves visiting non-French speakers. On the benevolent 'back-scratching' principle, why not? – *pourquoi pas?*

Learning the etiquette

Hand-shakes all round when meeting and leaving small groups of people, certainly when you're introduced for the first time, are *de rigueur*. Even if you missed out on a preliminary introduction and have not conversed with someone at all, a parting good-bye (and hallo) hand-shake goes down well! Meeting female company (working environments have their own rules) for the second time socially, within a short period of time, is the signal for exchange of cheek kisses: usually twice on each cheek in Paris, once on each cheek in the South of France, and sometimes three times in total in other parts of France. The *Tour de France* hostesses congratulate the winner of the day with a total of two or four kisses; three are rare. Family meetings mean kisses all round between all sexes.

Inevitably, certain people will be curious to know your origins and how such a thing is done in England. You will be expected to be the expert on all things English, and England is of course the UK. Even TV news announcers forget to make the distinction. So if you're a proud Scot and your accent has not passed you off as a *berrichon* (see above) you will have to put the record straight. The Scots, historically, have got on much better with the French than the English. If you are Welsh you may be asked exactly where Wales is. Not many French people know that Henry V, the victor of the French in the Hundred Years War Battle of Agincourt (*Azincourt*), was Welsh, although they all know that the English burnt Joan of Arc. (*Jeanne d'Arc – Légende et Vérité*, written by Manuel Gomez, a French journalist and published by Cheminements, does, however, try to prove that this is a mistaken belief.)

The neighbours

Inverted logic has it that the closer you are to neighbours the less you know them, except for closely knit village and rural communities. People living in blocks of flats with private balconies quite naturally don't want to be seen on their balconies if they can help it. Elaborate plants and trellises hide them from horizontally adjacent neighbours. You can hear them, but you won't see them and apart from flat owners' meetings you may go months without talking to them. The logic extends to houses with small gardens in little estates. In extreme cases fencing, sometimes subject to local limits, can barricade people in veritable fortresses. If you do not have a bell at the end of your front garden, even if your front gate is not locked, delivery men are so conditioned to expecting one that they wonder how to get in.

The solution to getting to know your neighbour is through their dog, child or their or somebody else's cat. All three are 'pet' subjects of conversation. An accompanied introduction to a neighbour's guard dog, be it a yapping poodle or angry alsatian, is also vital if you want a quiet life. Privacy is closely guarded. Immediate neighbours will sometimes telephone to ask you something rather than disturbing you with a personal appearance. Phoning after 8.30 am on weekdays, after 9 am on Saturdays, after 9.30 am on public holidays – avoid Christmas Day – and Sundays and on all days not later than 10 pm is acceptable.

Socialising

When you are invited to dinner with new friends, who probably won't be the neighbours, a present for the hostess is usual. This means flowers, a plant or something more personal. Wine is in order, especially champagne, as well as a lasting present if the host or hostess's birthday is being celebrated. Smart casual dress is appropriate – one-button-open tie-less shirts are quite acceptable – unless you and your wife have been invited to your boss's home for the first time for a formal dinner. Men can always dress down, removing jacket and tie, later on.

Shopping

France is undoubtedly the European leader in breadth and depth of products for sale, certainly for food and drink, through in- and out-of-town shopping centres, which first materialised at the end of the 1960s.

Food and drink

Mass-marketing (*la grande distribution*) through hypermarkets, supermarkets and mini-markets (*supérettes*) is mainly shared between the Auchan, Carrefour, Casino and Centre Leclerc retail groups, all of which expanded considerably throughout the 1970s. Auchan was founded in 1961 and Centre Leclerc, which is the most innovative and controversial mass-market retailer, opened shop in 1949. In recent years Leclerc have introduced in-store jewellery boutiques, bringing luxury products within the range of families shopping for more basic products and their publicity always emphasises attractive prices, giving them a deliberately down-market image.

Discount supermarkets appeared on the retail scene about 15 years ago and now nibble into the total retail cake at the rate of around one per cent a year, with approximately 17 per cent of the market at present. They have more limited ranges of products, pallet or open-carton displays, tight space between the display rows, less or non-existent voucher offers, and virtually no staff offering sample tasting. Price is all: at least ten per cent cheaper. Some products are identical to the more expensive ones, but in different packaging, as some 'discounters' are in the same central buying group as the traditional mass-market retailers. For example, Leader Price join forces with Casino, and Netto Hard Discount with Intermarchés supermarkets. Own-label discount supermarket products are naturally cheaper than comparable own-label mass-market retailers' products, for example bottled water.

Prices

Retail prices have been 'free' since 1986 and the government measures of the 1990s were largely unsuccessful in preventing the closing down of traditional village grocers. These measures included temporary freezes on new authorisations for hypermarkets and the 1996 *Loi Galland* (Galland's law) was designed to stop mass-market outlets undercutting small retail outlets on identical branded products by imposing a *minimum* retail price. Price *increases* suffered by customers were high on certain items, particularly since the introduction of the euro currency in 2002. Additionally, with voucher point systems and cumulative purchase offers, undercutting was *also* possible. It was often difficult to assess exactly what nett price was being paid by consumers. The *Loi Galland* is now being reviewed so that the price the customer pays will, in certain instances, reflect the huge discounts that mass-market retailers sometimes oblige their suppliers to give them for prime-position shelf space. Smaller retailers will no longer be protected. In September 2004 mass-market retailers reduced prices on 2,000 food lines by 1.6 per cent following an earlier agreement with the Minister of Finance.

Water

Domestic tap water is of course drinkable everywhere in France, but this cannot replace still, natural, spring water (*eau minérale naturelle plate*), particularly rich in magnesium and calcium, and naturally fizzy water which can have a pleasant salty flavour. Bottled water consumption is increasingly gaining ground to the detriment of wine consumption, particularly in restaurants.

Still, bottled water costs around half the price of fizzy water and can be bought in larger containers or bottles than fizzy water without affecting the taste once the seal has been broken. Look out for 5 litre bottles, like wine cartons, with an in-built tap.

Perrier is the 'Rolls Royce' of effervescent waters (*eaux gazeuses/eaux pétillantes*) – it is very fizzy and will give you a light spray if you get too close to it! – and costs about twice the price of the cheapest fizzy waters. The fizz is actually taken out of the water in the treatment process and then reintroduced. Some effervescent waters now have additional 'fizz' injected.

In an effort to attract children and newcomers to bottled water, most of the major brands now offer delicately flavoured lemon, strawberry, raspberry and orange waters in bottles ranging from small (25 cl) to family size (1.5 litre).

Wine

Bottled and carton wine are sold in all mass-market retailers, through independent wine retailers (*magasins de vins et spiritueux/cavistes*) who can give you specialist advice, and wine cooperatives (the Co-op system) who sell wine from the local vineyards. Cooperative wine is usually good value and so is wine bought during the wine promotion periods run by the big supermarket chains. Supermarkets have display boards giving general advice about wine to accompany different food.

Buying mail-order, especially if you bulk up your order for your medium-term requirements and/or make a bulk order with friends, is worthwhile. Make sure you've already tasted the wine. This can be a particularly good way to buy Champagne – the real thing is *always* marked 'Champagne' on the label – as acceptable Champagne is at least 15€ for a 75 cl bottle through retailers. A Champagne contact on the spot in the Champagne area should be treasured. Ensure you have tested dry (*brut*) and sweet (*doux*) Champagnes for your preference. And don't forget local wine fairs (*foires de vins*), or any other local food fairs for that matter, giving you the golden and free opportunity to test the local offerings before buying.

Rosé wine is often regarded by French people, unlike the British, as a 'hybrid' wine, a refreshing but not necessarily tasty accompaniment to summer pizzas and salads. Sales have in fact increased recently throughout France by 10 per cent.

Countless books have been published in French and English on wine and a small selection is given under Further Reading at the end of this book.

Cheese

The advent of hypermarkets and supermarkets has seen the reduction, through product rationalisation and mass pasteurisation production, of the number of cheeses available throughout France. General De Gaulle's statement *Nobody can simply bring together a country that has 265 kinds of cheese* no longer holds true... at least as far as the number of cheeses are concerned. The range is, however, still impressive. All mass-market retailers have a chilled, pre-packed, off-the-shelf selection, and most also have a cut-to-order (*au détail*) counter, and you will certainly find hard, soft and creamy cheeses that have not yet found their way to the UK. If old habits die hard and you still eat cheese in France at the end of the meal as well as before dessert, like everyone else, you will be thoroughly spoilt. Look out for fat content on the packaging (*... % matière grasse* or simply *...% MG*).

Traditional cheese shops (*fromageries*) selling just dairy products are now scarce, although you will find them in touristy villages and towns where the locally produced cheeses have earned their reputations through pungent taste or smells. If your French is adequate and there is a major library nearby, consult a facsimile copy of Brillat-Savarin's book *La Physiologie du Gout* (published 1826), a gastronomic bible which still holds good and lists the main cheeses of France and the best wines to drink with them. Some of the main French cheeses and their textures are listed below:

- Brie: soft;
- Camembert: soft;
- Cantal: hard;
- Comté: hard, like Gruyère;
- Fondu: soft;
- Munster: very strong, soft;
- Reblochon: semi-hard, strong;
- Roquefort: similar to Stilton;
- Tomme de Savoie, semi-hard;
- Vacherin: semi-soft, creamy.

Tea and coffee

If you really hanker after a 'strong cuppa tea' and can't get used to the specially diluted (for the French palate) English brands on sale in France you can now order the real thing online on the Best of British website: www.bestofbritish.fr or visit one of their shops if you're in Aix-en-Provence (in the Paradox English bookshop), Brive, Carcassonne, Civray, Confolens, Périgueux or Saint-Rémy-de-Provence. Most British jams, cereals, soups and preserves are available, and any good-sized supermarket will stock Weetabix and Worcester sauce.

With coffee more popular than tea in France – apparently it is also now in the UK – all self-respecting supermarkets will have a choice of mild to stronger pack filter coffees in 250 gram single packs. Semi-professional espresso coffee machines which turn out beautiful coffee from a variety of individually packed coffee doses are tempting, but can work out to be an expensive luxury if you drink four or five coffees a day. A good compromise for those who look for taste in their coffee at a reasonable price is the recently marketed Philips Senseo percolator which produces a first-class coffee from standard-size circular individual coffee bags. Look out for tasting demonstrations in hypermarkets and individual coffee bag packs supplied by various coffee companies. If you already have a Senseo machine you will be pleasantly surprised to find that French individual coffee bags work out around 35 per cent cheaper than their UK equivalents.

Bread

It came as quite a shock to some Parisian bakers recently that an appraisal of some 600 standard baguettes from 600 bakers' shops was set out in a guide written by an *American* in Paris. The classic baguette weighing 200 grams costs around 00.60€ and in some remote rural areas is still delivered by bakers to households.

If you want your baguette straight from the oven ask for *bien cuite* (well-done) or *pas trop bien cuite* (not too well-done) around 7.30 am for breakfast, and around 7 pm for the evening meal. Most supermarkets with their own bread ovens will have a separate baker's counter for all sorts of fresh bread which include *pain au son* (bran bread) and *pain de seigle* (rye bread). You can ask for bread to be sliced in a machine, at no extra cost, if you want it for toast. If you're after a British type of tin loaf for toast go to the shelves of pre-packed bread and look for sliced *pain de mie* which comes in white or wholemeal (*complet*) varieties. You will also find rye bread bloomer-shaped sliced loaves. Hypermarkets often also have film-wrapped baguette which is worth buying for a small emergency stock in the freezer.

Fish

Fresh fish counters with a fishmonger in attendance to serve, sell and advise are standard in supermarkets and hypermarkets. If you want a market atmosphere, traditional fishmongers' shops and fishermen selling their mornings' catch in port straight off their boats are more lively. Butchers in supermarkets are more rare, although a variety of joints of meat, sufficient for most tastes, are cut and packaged by an army of butchers behind the scenes. If you want special advice or special cuts it is best go to the local butcher, although you will pay more.

Shopping locally

Regional specialities range from pastries and cakes to candied fruits *(fruits confits)* and preserved game such as wild boar *(sanglier)* in a rich sauce, packed in long-life sealed jars. They are made using recipes handed down through generations for which you will pay a premium price, regardless of whether they are now produced on a small scale or in mass-production factories. Special regional or local product displays *(produits régionaux)* have all-year round display shelving in prominent positions in mass-market retailers. Speciality shops such as *fromageries* (see above) sometimes offer regional products which are prepared on the premises. Certainly worth trying and you only risk becoming addicted.

For quality fresh vegetables and fruit, enjoy shopping in the town or village market for local produce which won't have suffered from the transport and refrigeration chain of *la grande distribution*. Going one stage further than buying direct from the farm is the increasingly popular pre-paid standing order system which guarantees you fresh produce from a local farm, without necessarily knowing what products will be available. You do have to rely on the judgement of the farmer who plans the crop, so a first-hand recommendation is advisable.

Clothes

Department stores *(grands magasins)* such as Printemps and Galeries Lafayette, boutiques and hypermarkets offer a tremendously rich range of clothes in all categories and at all prices. If designer labels are not your priority, well-tailored and styled quality clothes can be bought off-the-peg, in department stores and boutiques, at prices which are generally less than for similar products in the UK.

Trouser lengths for men vary with waist sizes and tend to be enormously long. Most clothes shops offer a trouser-leg trimming and sewing service (*service ourlet*) included in the price tag or for a nominal amount. Low-price stores and street markets won't offer the *service ourlet*. They receive continual new deliveries of assorted new clothes (*lots*) and are worth visiting regularly. *Beware of designer label clothes offered in markets at ridiculously low prices.* They are probably illegal copies and customer ignorance of this fact is no excuse in the eyes of the law. There are heavy fines.

Men spend more on clothes than women in the officially set sales (*soldes*) periods in winter and summer, confirming that men will accept the previous season's styles in stock clearances more easily than women. Best discounts are up to 50 per cent off. In practice sales goods are not changed or refunded if they don't fit so make sure they do, but if they have a defect which was not obvious (*viche caché*) when bought they should be refunded. For obvious reasons, buying clothes at closing down sales (*soldes de liquidation*), which must be authorised by the local prefecture, is a little risky even if you've carefully chosen the article.

Useful vocabulary

bien cuite (pas trop)	well-done (but not too much)
brut	dry (champagne and cider)
doux	sweet (wine)
eau gazeuse/pétillante	effervescent water
eau plate	still water
élevé en plein air	free-range (chicken etc)
fruits confits	candied fruits
grands magasins	department stores
grande distribution	mass-marketing
pain complet	wholemeal bread
pain de mie	sandwich/toast bread
pain de seigle	rye bread
produits congelés/surgelés	frozen foods
sanglier	wild boar
sec	dry (wine)

soldes	sale
solde de liquidation	closing down sale
superette	mini-market

Buying cars and durable household goods

If the model you buy has a short guarantee, say under three years, it is worth extending this to at least three years for a comparatively reasonable supplement to the sale price. After the guarantee has expired it makes good sense to take the car for specific repairs to the nearest garage (*agent*) that deals with your make of car. This may not be the area dealer (*concessionnaire*) where you originally bought the car and they may even be more expensive. However, they offer the flexibility that a larger garage will not provide, particularly for local customers. Oil-change and filter replacement servicing (*vidanges*), as opposed to mechanical repairs, are reasonably priced at while-you-wait garages whose main business is often tyre repair and sales.

- Secondhand cars over four years old must be sold with a valid MOT certificate (*certificat de controle technique*) whether buying through a dealer or privately. There is a two-month period immediately following the test in which any required repairs must be carried out. If you are buying or selling a car with certain repairs to be done following the test these must be pointed out.

- The *controle technique* test is every two years following the initial test for new cars after four years. Although the majority of cars are increasingly well maintained by drivers (see How to Drive in this chapter) the 18 to 25 age group still have a reputation for punishing cars as they drive recklessly. If a car has at some stage had a bad crash a potential buyer must be informed.

The *Glass's Guide* equivalent to secondhand car prices is the *Argus de l'automobile* which gives secondhand prices based on an annual average of 20,000 kilometres. It also carries car sale ads and has useful information for both buyers and sellers.

Buying household goods

Replacing or buying new furniture, household appliances, gardening and DIY tools can be a difficult chore. Nearly all out-of-town shopping centres, trading estates or industrial estates will contain a garden centre, DIY and building materials store and several furniture shops. The choice is overwhelming.

For sports equipment the choice is easier. The Decathlon chain has almost a monopoly out-of-town, and the sales people can give you first-hand advice as they practise the sport for which they sell the equipment.

Electrical goods

Relatively high-cost electrical appliances which are used daily such as refrigerators, cookers, dish and clothes washing machines will have the manufacturer's or store's two-year guarantee, although they should of course last at least five years. It is worth considering paying for an additional three-year guarantee for which the cost – check the contract – can be offset against a new purchase when the guarantee runs out, provided you have not had to make a claim against the guarantee. Electrical goods wholesalers (*grossistes en appareils d'électroménager*) usually make their 'privileged' membership cards available to anyone who has a valid credit card. The Darty electrical goods and multi-media equipment retail chain stores have attractively laid out displays, excellent and courteous sales people and, above all, a prompt and reliable after-sales service (*service après vente: SAV*). As they have a standard call-out rate to your home it may be worth taking small items, such as video recorders (*magnétoscopes*) into their *SAV* depot if it is nearby.

Reconditioned secondhand appliances with a guarantee (*électroménager recyclé et garanti*) or, even better, new slightly marked goods – 'seconds' (*électroménager de second choix*) – with the original guarantee are worth considering if your property is mainly used for holidays or if your purchase was made with a quick resale in mind, especially as in the latter case capital gains tax (*l'impôt sur le plus-value*) will be levied.

Most stores selling household appliances will refund you the difference if you find the identical branded product cheaper elsewhere. In practice, you cannot normally find an identical cheaper product elsewhere as they either have an own-brand label or are the exclusive distributor in the locality.

Quality assurance

Price and guarantee are settled but the problems of quality and security remain. All products sold of course are subject to European standards. The *norme française: NF* label stuck onto articles or their packaging is not obligatory, but 90 per cent of French people (who generally expect nothing but perfection) are reassured by it. The old 'made in France' label is no longer possible for many goods which are now manufactured in South-East Asia, but *NF* means that the products have been tested and their factories inspected for quality, safety and suitability for the French customer's needs. (The *NF* label is also extending to passenger transport companies and holiday camping sites where safety is a vital consideration.)

Durable goods, environmentally friendly products, food and drink products and services are all covered by *NF* labels. There are also specialised labels certifying quality for goods such as double-glazing, the *Acotherm* label, *A2P* for alarm systems, and the *CST Bat* certificate for new building techniques and products.

Buying on the internet

Approximately five million people in France now buy something every year on an internet shopping site. On-line shopping, sometimes with product application details for gardening, building and practical goods, is offered by major store groups. Mail order shopping (*vente par correspondence: VPC*) which has a long history in France continues to be an important way to shop. Leading catalogue companies are *La Redoute* and *3 Suisses* who have built their reputations on quality products and reliable deliveries. Consumer law gives mail order customers the possibility of returning goods within seven days of receipt for a complete refund if they have a change of heart: no questions asked. (To avoid this inconvenience for bulky furniture items, a visit before ordering to the company's showroom makes sense if there is one in your area.) If the goods are faulty or are not what were ordered the mail order company also pays the return transport.

Useful vocabulary

appareils électroménagers	household appliances
bricolage	DIY
certificat de contrôle technique	MOT certificate
grossiste	wholesaler
magnétoscope	video recorder
service après vente: SAV	after sales service
vente par correspondence	mail order

Publications

Although France has noticeably fewer daily national newspapers than the UK, television makes up for this with three national and international news programmes on the three main channels, each of which lasts at least 30 minutes daily. With the regional daily press there are, in fact, slightly more titles published daily in France than in the UK. Overall the French read fewer newspapers daily than in the UK: around 13 million copies compared with around 20 million printed daily in the UK.

There is a choice of several competitive magazines and periodicals on the same subjects and the total number published is probably more than in the UK. An interesting peculiarity is that crossword magazines of various grades of difficulty are extremely popular.

Regular information spots on TV advise you on your basic rights regarding matters relating to credit agreements, house purchases, private estate regulations etc, and what and when to eat to stay fit and healthy. Consumer magazine editors are also interviewed, giving advice on what to choose when buying durable consumer goods. *Que Choisir* and the Institut National de la Consommation's *60 Millions de Consommateurs* are the two leading magazines. The monthly magazine *Dossier Familial* which contains a variety of surveys on financial and practical matters concerning family life claims to have the largest magazine subscription figure in France at 1.4 million.

Most English newspapers are available in major cities in France all year and in tourist areas in the tourist seasons. With the exception of *The Guardian*, the *Times* and the *Daily Mail*, which are printed in France and available on publication day, British newspapers arrive on news-stands the day after publication. The American daily newspaper *International Herald Tribune*, which is slightly cheaper than the above mentioned British daily newspapers, is also sold on publication day because it is printed in France. Subscriptions reduce the annual cost considerably, but if you are not in a major town delivery on publication day is not guaranteed.

Advertising

While total advertising spending in the UK is supposedly almost twice that of France's, radio advertising, street signs and posters in France are much more important than in the UK. There are also around 500 free-sheets published regularly throughout the whole of France and household letter-boxes in any urban area receive two or three every week, along with a host of bumf, almost daily, mainly from large stores and hypermarkets. If you can organise your reading time efficiently there are good buys to be found. A large *pas de publicité* sign on your letter-box if you're often absent will prevent an overflow situation which is a sure indication to burglars that you're away.

You are inevitably canvassed on the phone by *télé-marketing* people even if your surname begins with a Z. Play the foreigner if you want to get rid of them quickly and bear in mind that you have a seven-day 'cooling-off' period if you order something following a cold-call appointment and/or visit to your home.

How to drive

Sanctions for violating the Highway Code (*Code de la Route*) have been strictly applied since 2002, including the drinking and driving law and the recent driving-under-the-influence-of-drugs law. Road deaths have as a result been reduced remarkably by 20 per cent. A discernible change in drinking and driving habits is gaining ground, mainly because of the fines (*amendes*) incurred and points penalty system (see below) and not because drivers are prepared to accept the idea that speeding and/or drinking and driving are dangerous. Supposedly intelligent people still claim that they know how to handle their drink even though scientific evidence shows that reaction time is impaired. Others claim that the application of the democratically voted law is an infringement of their personal liberty. Late-night drivers in quiet rural areas, particularly in the 18–25 age group, still take risks forgetting that other drivers may be on the roads.

Respect the regulations and be wary of other drivers, cyclists, adolescents on motor scooters *and* pedestrians. Pedestrians who have never driven are sometimes quite oblivious to crossing roads safely. Particular driving and pedestrian situations to be wary of are:

- **Traffic lights**. Pedestrians crossing when they are green for drivers. Drivers going through red lights or not knowing when they turn to green because they've braked at the last moment and have partly overshot the lights.

- **Pedestrian crossings**. Being on the pavement as a pedestrian giving a definite indication that you want to cross does not mean that cars will stop. Being on the pedestrian crossing is no guarantee either. However, anyone pushing a pram or pushchair will invariably get cars to stop. You may even be insulted as an adult – minus pushchair or pram – if you don't acknowledge the 'courtesy' of drivers when they do stop or slow down so that you can cross. As a driver give the person behind you plenty of time to stop when you stop at pedestrian crossings. The same applies for traffic lights.

- **Motorways**. Occasionally two motorways merge without a 'give way' indication. Best to get on the overtaking lane ie the left-hand lane if you're on the motorway to the left, thus avoiding the lanes which merge, and if you're on the motorway to the right, move over to the right-hand lane. Remember when overtaking on motorways to pull back in to the right-hand lane as soon as it's safe to do so. Hogging the middle line is an offence.

  Give yourself plenty of time to slow down before taking a motorway exit. Motorway speed signs drop quickly from 130 kph to exit road and urban 50 kph signs. Exit roads often have tight bends as well.

- **Towns**. 50 kph is the maximum speed permitted in urban areas. Well signposted, this may drop suddenly to 30 kph, which will be signposted, near schools, hospitals, public parks, etc. Don't get caught out if you don't know the area.

- **Shopping centre car parks**. There is no official right of way in these car parks. What should be a no-hassle driving area can be the scene of minor incidents as bad driving habits come into their own. No one can say who is right or wrong unless a one-way sign is not respected. The standard *Constat Européen de déclaration d'accident* form (the standard car insurance accident declaration form to be completed and signed by drivers involved in a minor accident) has little weight here. Grab witnesses.

- **Keep your distance**. With so many people driving up to or exceeding the speed limits, and overtaking drivers who are below these speeds, it is difficult to keep an emergency-stop safe distance between cars in front of and behind you. Watch out also for temporary postmen filling in during the holiday season, steering their mopeds with one hand, answering their mobile phones and looking for addresses, simultaneously! On a positive note, you are unlikely to get stuck behind smelly dustcarts during the day. Most collections are done around dawn.

- **Roundabouts**. These have flourished in recent years and urban area roundabouts seem to be in perpetual competition for the roundabout with the most-flourishing-and-highest-plants-and flowers award. Small drivers in Minis have a problem seeing what's coming onto the opposite entrance to the roundabout. Elderly French drivers once on a roundabout often still give way to traffic coming onto the roundabout from the right. Old habits die hard. Traffic on the roundabout has right of way.

Rules and regulations

Since 1992 there has been a points penalty system which deducts points from 12-point driving licences. There are five categories (*classes*) of offences; one, two, three, four and six-point individual offences; fines up to 9,000€, three year driving licence suspension and possible imprisonment for two or three years depending on the gravity of a driving under the influence of drink/drugs offence. Driving accidents causing death are liable to at least a five-year prison sentence.

Details and explanation of the points system are given (in French) on the www.permis-a-points.com website. Some French ferry ports hand out leaflets in English to disembarking drivers with guidelines to driving in France.

Drivers who have just obtained their driving licence now receive a six-point driving licence with the possibility of obtaining a 12-point licence after two years.

A further measure in 2003 was the introduction of automatic radar speed traps on many major roads throughout France. Six points are deducted from licences for driving 50 kph above a speed limit. The holder of the *carte grise* (vehicle's log book) is, logically, financially responsible for fines even though they may not have been driving. Make sure anyone you lend your car to has, of course, a driving licence – look at the points situation – drives sensibly and is financially viable.

Always have your insurance certificate sticker and *contrôle technique* sticker displayed on the front windscreen and your licence and *carte grise* on you. Police expect these to be produced immediately whenever they carry out spot checks (*contrôle de papiers*) and you will need them to fill out the *Constat Européen de déclaration d'accident* form in the event of an accident. It is also advisable as a foreigner to have additional ID on you. Most French people carry their identity card with them.

Useful vocabulary

amende	fine
carte grise	log book
permis de conduire	driving licence

Living healthily

The superb health system in France, which for years has been increasingly running into the red, provides in most areas a choice of general practitioners and immediate access to blood-test laboratories.

Eating healthily is the subject of a free comprehensive government booklet (in French only), *La Santé Vient en Mangeant*, which recommends the daily consumption of at least five different fruits and vegetables; potatoes, beans or other pulses, bread or cereals at each meal; three dairy products; small quantities of fish, meat or eggs – with fish at least twice a week; limited amounts of fatty foods, preferably of vegetable extraction; and a limited amount of chocolate, cakes and sweets, avoiding food that has both fat and sugar content. Education starts at an early age: some *mutuelle* (complementary health assurance) companies distribute educative packs of happy family cards with dairy products, fatty products, fruit and vegetable, meat – fish – eggs, cereals, and water families. *La Santé Vient en Mangeant* officially tolerates wine consumption with up to three 10 cl glasses a day for men and two for women. The alcohol content of a tumbler (*un demi*) of normal strength beer is equivalent to that of a 10 cl glass of wine. However, if you are teetotal or drink only occasionally, starting to drink alcohol or increasing your intake is not recommended officially!

The recently introduced health measures are aimed at reducing financial wastage through 'unnecessary' visits and consultations, providing more effective health-care and eliminating fraud. These are:

* 1€ retained by the social security system every time you visit your doctor;

* a visit to your usual GP (*médecin généraliste-traitant*) before consulting a specialist unless you're prepared to pay more by visiting a specialist directly (eye specialists, gynaecologists, neurologists, psychiatrists and paediatricians excepted and also visits to specialists if you're away from home and your GP);

- a computerised central data bank from 2007 containing patients' medical information and from 2006 a *Vitale* health card (*carte d'assurance maladie*) displaying a photo of the holder.

All salaried employees, from the age of 16, have the right to a complete and free check-up every five years in a health test centre (*Centre d'Examens de Santé*). This covers the heart, blood pressure, hearing, eyesight, vaccinations, weight, teeth and dental care, a urine and comprehensive blood test, colonic/prostate/breast/lung/cervical cancer tests with immediate X-rays, if considered necessary, etc. Additionally, a quick annual check-up is provided for salaried employees by the *Médecin du Travail*.

Health care costs

France is the leading European nation for per capita consumption of medicines. Since 1999 chemists (*pharmaciens*) have been allowed to suggest medicines (*medicaments génériques*) with no registered trademark which are identical to the branded medicine prescribed, unless the prescription states that a substitute is not acceptable. You are not obliged to accept the suggestion. Savings to the health service are between 30 to 40 per cent. France is a long way behind the UK where more than 50 per cent of medicines now taken are not registered trademarks. In April 2003 the standard rate of health service reimbursement in France on 617 prescribed medicines was reduced from 65 to 35 per cent. Some 'non-essential' pills which may be prescribed by your GP for a regular course of treatment to give more comfort are not reimbursed at all. It can pay to shop around *pharmaciens* whose minimum prices are not fixed as price variation for exactly the same product can be considerable.

Seventy per cent of the cost fixed by the government of a visit to a GP (*médecin généraliste*), apart from the 1€ supplement, is reimbursed by the state provided you pay social security contributions. Visits to specialists, whose fees are naturally higher, and are not fixed, are also reimbursed on the same percentage basis, but off a higher consultation fee fixed by the government. Most patients take out additional health cover through a *mutuelle* company, the great majority of which reimburse the total difference of 30 per cent. The portion of a specialist's fee above the Ministry of Health figure is not reimbursed by *mutuelle* cover. *Mutuelle* policy premiums depend on age at entry and precise cover offered which also covers hospitalisation and dental care, but only part of the material cost of new teeth (see final paragraph). Investment in *mutuelle* cover is strongly recommended. GPs also prescribe blood tests, on request, once or twice a year or more often if they judge necessary, which are carried out in a *Laboratoire de Biologie Médicale/d'Analyes Médicales*. These are reimbursed on the same basis as visits to GPs. Free medical cover (*Couverture maladie universelle: CMU*) has been available since 2000 for people able to prove particularly low resources and who have been resident in France for at least three months.

The European health card, introduced in June 2004, now provides immediately necessary as well as emergency medical treatment cover for temporary EC visitors.

Only around 25 per cent of the cost of manufacturing replacement ceramic teeth is reimbursed and a standard clause in a *mutuelle* policy will limit the amount in any one year. If you wish to obtain the maximum social security reimbursement rate of 65 per cent for glasses, low-cost standard 'national health' lenses and frames, which are not unattractive, are available. An eye specialist's report is of course necessary. Glasses for children under 6 years old are free and there are generous allowances for the 6–18 age group.

Useful vocabulary

Vitale carte d'assurance maladie	National Health card for reimbursements
médicaments génériques	medicines without registered trademarks
médecin généraliste	GP
mutuelle	company providing complementary health cover
pharmacien	chemist

6
Your Rights and the Law

Nationals of member countries of the European Community who reside in France cannot vote in national elections, need special authorisation to enter military bases and cannot be employed in local government and the civil service. However, nearly all other areas of activity are open to them.

A residence permit is necessary if you stay for more than three consecutive months. Apply to the town hall in small communities and, in large towns, to the *service des étrangers* at the national police station (*commissariat*). When renewing these, every ten years, allow a few months for the new *carte* to be issued, although you will be issued with a temporary certificate covering any overlap period. The plastic-coated ID card now protects your photo so that you are recognisable: a great improvement on previous cards, when it was not unknown to be asked for a second ID document!

The information contained in this chapter has been chosen for the situations that are most likely to concern you. This information can be supplemented by free consultations, by appointment, with the following:

- a solicitor (*avocat*) at a *Maison de la Justice et du Droit* who will confirm, for example, if you have grounds for litigation;

- a state *médiateur* (a sort of ombudsman), arranged via the local MP or senator, who will assist you in cases of difficulty, dispute or disagreement with a local public or government organisation;

- a *conciliateur* (mediator) arranged through the town hall, if you have a disagreement with a private person such as your neighbour, in the interests of finding common ground for an amicable agreement;

- the area Fair Trading Office (*Concurrence, Consommation et Repression des Fraudes – direction régionale et départementale*) if you feel you have been subject to fraud or swindled.

This list is not exhaustive. You can also use your Embassy or Consulate to point you in the right direction. They may also be able to give you some guidelines. Some notary offices display free leaflets on inheritance, wills and property matters.

Civic obligations

Pets

Although vaccination of pets is only obligatory in officially declared rabies areas, it is strongly recommended. Reputable breeders' advertisements always confirm that dogs have been vaccinated. Dangerous dogs, such as pit bull terriers, must be muzzled and kept on a leash in public. A prison sentence is possible for cruelty to pets.

Children

In a similar vein to pet vaccinations, schoolchildren suffering from smallpox, scarlet fever or worse must respect minimum periods of absence from school. Children must be educated at school between the ages of 6 and 16, so rare but necessary absences are unlikely to hamper scholastic progress.

Tax

If you pay income tax in France and realise, afterwards, that you have made a mistake in the completion of your income declaration form you have up until the end of the calendar year following the year of the declaration to send in a *déclaration rectificative* pointing out the error with the corrected figure and/or information. The same applies to any claim you wish to lodge if you consider your tax amount (*avis d'imposition*) to be incorrect. The original income declaration form must have been sent in by the due date unless you wish to incur a tax surcharge which starts off at ten per cent. In the event of a tax inspection by the income tax authorities they must inform the person concerned beforehand of their rights and obligations (*droits et obligations*) as an inspected taxpayer.

Crime

An important citizen's duty as a witness to any accident or crime involving danger to fellow citizen(s) is to alert the police, fire brigade or ambulance service or to 'have a go' yourself if neither you nor anybody else is at risk. Failure to do so runs the risk of a five-year prison sentence. Immediate family apart, not informing the police about criminal activities and planned crimes is punishable by three years' imprisonment and a hefty fine.

The State's obligations

A major change in French law in 2000 was the introduction of the presumption of innocence, throwing the burden of finding proof or conclusive arguments on to the prosecutor. It is advisable to register with your Embassy or local Consulate to speed up any official assistance you may require if you do, unwittingly, run foul of the law.

Despite the precautions and enquiries made at time of purchase, a private property may subsequently become subject to a compulsory purchase order in the public interest. Laid-down administrative (the enquiry) and judicial procedures must be respected and a fair price paid before the owner has to move.

The state can now indemnify anyone who normally resides in France or any other EU country for physical injuries which are suffered as a direct result of a terrorist or other violent attack.

In the case of poorly maintained roads or roads under repair with inadequate warning signs the financial liability for any resulting accident will lie either with the police, state, *département* or motorway company, depending on the category of road – national, motorway, departmental or municipal. Proving who is responsible may be another matter.

EC nationals' voting rights

The 36,000 mayors in France wield considerable power in their community. They have wide-ranging responsibilities – they are *de facto* head of the local police (*police municipale*) – and can also be held personally liable for accidents resulting from poor maintenance of municipal buildings if it can be shown that mismanagement or negligence is their fault. Mayors with a strong following in the council team (*conseillers municipaux*) can transform their community in the space of one six-year mandate and it is not unknown for them to be at loggerheads with the mayor in the adjacent community over boundary matters.

For all these reasons it makes sense for foreigners to exercise their right to vote in the municipal elections. The next elections will be in 2007.

Voting for European MPs (*députés européens*) is also open to resident EC nationals. The 2004 elections still only attracted 50 per cent of the electorate. With the explosion of the European Community to 25 members in 2004 their future importance is evident.

To vote in both these elections, registration on the electoral roll must follow a minimum period of six months of continuous residence in the community. First-time registration must be made between September and December.

Legal responsibility

Under civil law you can be pursued by anyone claiming damages against you whether your actions were deliberately or negligently caused. Accident insurance covers children, animals, machinery, buildings, etc for whom or which you are responsible.

As with speeding offences committed by someone who is using your car (see How to Drive in Chapter 5), you are financially responsible for any injuries caused to a third party by someone who has been invited to your property if they are not the joint-owner or lessee of the property. A point to bear in mind if you regularly receive friends. Make sure you have appropriate insurance cover.

People who are not invited are also concerned. If a trespasser drowns in your swimming pool you may be responsible. Permanent swimming pools now being installed in properties and existing permanent swimming pools in rented properties must have a surrounding security barrier of at least 1.10 m high, or an intrusion alarm system or a solid impenetrable cover. Existing permanent pools in private properties, which are not rented out from time to time, must comply with this regulation by the beginning of 2006.

Hoteliers *are* responsible under civil law for guests' possessions left in rooms for up to a value of 100 times the daily room rate and for the total value if they're consigned to the hotel's safe, despite any room notices denying responsibility. They are also responsible for cars left in the hotel's car park and for up to the value of 50 times the daily room rate for any articles stolen from cars. Armed robbery is, however, a valid defence for a hotel. This doesn't mean that due care and attention should not be taken with valuables left in hotel rooms. Lack of appropriate security may also be grounds for compensation claims if personal injuries are involved. At the time of writing a British couple were suing a hotel chain for the equivalent of over £2 million for physical and psychological damage following a toxic gas robbery.

For general information, breach of the law is judged under three categories.

1   *Contraventions punies d'amendes* (fineable offences). *Contraventions* can no longer be sanctioned by a prison sentence. Those *contraventions* which go to court are judged by a *tribunal d'instance* which in effect is a police court for fines.

2   *Délit* (misdemeanour). This covers theft, fraud, manslaughter etc. Misdemeanours incur imprisonment or a heavy fine depending on the nature and gravity of the law-breaking act. They are judged by three judges before a *tribunal correctional*. Courts have a heavy back-log of cases awaiting trial. This is why in October 2004 the Minister of Justice, M. Perben, introduced his 'plead guilty' law giving people who had already declared their guilt, when arrested, the opportunity of not having to be tried before a court. Misdemeanours punishable before a court with up to five years in gaol now only incur a sentence of up to one year under the 'plead guilty' option.

3   *Crime* (felony). Judgement is before a *cour d'assizes*. Guilt is always punished by a prison sentence.

Maternity rights and benefits

France and Ireland hold the highest European birth-rate: just under two children per family.

Despite the recent reform to the state pension system, meaning that millions of people will in the future have to work longer before reaching retirement, France still needs more births, principally to provide a larger future working force to pay for the increased financial demands on the system from already retired people, or those now coming up for retirement, who are living longer and longer.

Maternity entitlements and nationality

The maternity entitlements below apply if you reside, work and pay social security contributions in France.

- You can ask for French nationality for your child, born in France, assuming neither parent is French, and with the child's agreement, from the age of 13. A total of five years' previous residence is required. The child will automatically conserve their British nationality if you are British. They will be treated officially as French in France and British in the UK. The best of both worlds.

- Maternity leave (*congé de maternité*), if requested, is obligatory on full pay with employment held over. Even the smallest companies, where this may create a staffing problem, are included. For the first or second child a total of 16 weeks is given: six before the due date and ten after. From the third child onwards leave is extended to 18 weeks. The entitlement for twins, logically, more than doubles first or second child maternity leave to 34 weeks, and if you do better than that 46 weeks is allowed.

- Absence for medical examinations and limited extensions to these leave periods, on production of a doctor's certificate, without loss of pay are permitted.

- Fathers are entitled to two weeks' paternity leave on 80 per cent of gross salary, limited to around 840€.

- Any salaried person who has worked in the same company for at least one year when the child is born can benefit from unpaid extended post-natal maternity (or paternity) leave (*congé parental d'éducation*) from their employer or part-time work (under certain conditions) with full-time previous employment held over. The employer must be officially notified by registered letter with an acknowledgement of receipt form (*lettre recommandée avec accusé de réception*). This continuous leave can be extended until the child is three years old, although there have been recent discussions about possibly reducing this period.

- If you or the other parent have given up work entirely following the birth of at least a second child a post-natal maternity or paternity allowance (*allocation parentale d'éducation: APE*) is paid during the extended post-natal maternity leave until the last born child is three years old. The parent concerned must have worked for at least two years in the previous five years in the case of a two child family and for at least two years in the previous ten years in the case of a larger family. The flat rate grant up to end of June 2005 was 515.21€ per month per family.

Family allowances

The state family allowance (*allocation familiale: AF*) is paid to all families, regardless of resources, with at least two children. It was 115.64€ a month up to June 2005 for two-children families, shooting up to 263.80€ per month for three-children families – France needs more children – with an additional 148€ per month for each further child.

Parents working part-time, if they work fewer than 28 hours a week, may be entitled to the *complement de libre choix d'activité* allowance. This is granted subject to income.

Details of all parental allowances are given on the national family allowances information website www.cnaf.fr (click on *toutes les prestations*) or visit, and wait your turn, in the nearest *Caisse d'Allocations Familiales (CAF)* office.

Using solicitors

If the available free consultations listed at the beginning of this chapter do not resolve your problem you may have to use a solicitor. In divorce, for example, an official act has to be drawn up and litigation dealt with by representation in court or a solicitor's letter.

Specialised problems are best settled using a specialist solicitor who can, since 1990, show their speciality on business cards or plaques in their offices providing this is not construed as touting for business.

Solicitors' fees, apart from certain at-cost fees for use of a bailiff (*huissier*), travel expenses, translations, etc are negotiable. *Before* instructing a solicitor, come to an agreement, or go elsewhere if you are not in agreement, on their fees and give your instruction in writing. A 15 minute consultancy and a solicitor's registered letter to your adversary can cost around 250€ which includes 19.6 per cent VAT. Small practices may be exempt from paying VAT. Time, complexity and the advantage you will gain from using their services are all factors to be taken into account in establishing fees. Complexity, for example, could be judged in the case of a solicitor who acts as an interpreter because he speaks French, English and Greek when dealing with your adversary who only speaks Greek. Not to be confused with translation of a document. A solicitor may, quite legally, ask you to pay in cash, although they cannot insist on this. Whether you pay in cash or by cheque make sure you receive a 'paid' invoice detailing what you are paying for.

If you are claiming money due to you a solicitor may ask for ten per cent of the settlement amount if the affair is settled in or out of court through them. You may be able to settle the affair directly following a solicitor's initial letter. A fee to 'close your file' (*solder le dossier*) may then be claimed. If copies, certified by the town hall free of charge as being copies, of original documents are left with the solicitor from the outset, the act of closing the file should not be necessary.

Recommendations are invaluable. A solicitor who has successfully handled a similar problem at a reasonable price is to be treasured, as is a friendly retired solicitor who may offer advice as a favour, although they cannot act officially.

Partial or total legal aid (*aide juridictionnelle*) is your right if your monthly income is below certain amounts fixed on a sliding scale. For an application made in 2004 (through the town hall or a *tribunal de grande instance*), monthly income in 2003 below 830€ qualified for total financial aid. If you or your immediate family have been subject to any form of physical attack you are entitled to legal aid, regardless of your income. In civil law matters, a solicitor who is prepared to accept the set fees paid to them by the state for representing a legal aid client in court may be difficult to find. If you qualify for legal aid it is best to first of all find a solicitor who will take on your case.

Using notaries

Notaires, unlike *avocats*, are public officers who therefore must have French nationality, and are appointed by the Minister of Justice. In the interests of public service these appointments are made according to the size of your local community. A large town will have several practices while a medium-sized village will have one, or perhaps none at all. There are around 8,000 notaries in France for approximately 35,000 communities. You can of course use a notary who is not in your community. In the case of property purchase it is usual to use just the seller's *notaire*.

While *notaires* are self-employed, running private practices (*études*), most contracts and documents they draw up and authenticate, such as marriage contracts setting out property and goods entitlement of both spouses, wills, financial settlements and property sale deeds, have fixed or sliding-scale remuneration rates (*émoluments*). The notary must inform you of their remuneration beforehand for any contract or preparation of an official document not subject to a set rate. Chapter 4 refers to conveyancing costs and taxes for property purchase and the sliding scale notary fees (*honoraires*) if you also use a notary as an estate agent.

Honoraires for expert notary advice or consultation on matters such as family and property settlements are, however, negotiable. Ask for a costing beforehand. As this is an area where both solicitors and notaries can give advice you may get a better deal through a notary if they anticipate instruction for an official contract following your visit. Authenticated wills and financial settlements between spouses, and property completion sales deeds, can only be drawn up by notaries.

Insurance

Since freedom of commercial choice really came into effect in the EC at the end of 1993 there is no reason why insurance policies cannot be taken out with companies anywhere in Europe. For practical reasons it makes sense to have a local office within striking distance if you need to complain effectively. (Norwich Union, now known in France as *Aviva*, have in fact had French offices or agents – *agents généraux* – for around 100 years.)

Obligatory insurance providing at least third party cover applies to all motorised vehicles driven anywhere. If you are employed or self-employed you must pay contributions into the French social security system unless you have been seconded to France by a foreign company or unless you're allowed to register the headquarters of your own company outside France. Household contents insurance policies with a French company usually specify that front doors must have at least three locking points so this should be checked if an old property is being bought for restoration. Window shutters should also be closed at night to provide insurance cover.

It is strongly recommended (see Legal Responsibility above) to take out insurance cover against accidents or incidents caused by people and materials for whom you are responsible.

The following general points apply to any French insurance policy:

- **Immediate cover**. Ask for a *note de couverture* which will be replaced subsequently by the official policy (*police d'assurance*).

- **Cancellation possibility** (*droit de résiliation*). If a policy has just been taken out which is valid for at least two months, ie most policies, it can be cancelled by registered letter within 30 days of having made the first premium payment. Total reimbursement is due within 30 days of cancellation.

The insurance company themselves can also reserve the right to cancel a policy, after a claim, in certain circumstances. Motor vehicle insurance policy cancellations are excluded unless the driver has their licence suspended or withdrawn or is guilty of a drink/drug offence.

- **Premium payments**. If you don't sign a direct debit authorisation form you have a maximum of ten days over the due monthly or annual payment date in which to pay. The insurance company can temporarily suspend cover 30 days after having sent you a registered letter after the ten-day period and advise cancellation of the policy (which will take effect 40 days after this letter).

Marriage, divorce and inheritance

You may have married in the UK, but if you decide to divorce in France you will of course be subject to French law and will have to pay the additional charge of having your marriage lines translated by an authorised translator of official documents (*traducteur assermenté*).

If you decide to marry in France and then change your mind, a substantiated breach of contract (*promesse de marriage*) is still grounds for legal proceedings if your ex future partner is so inclined. Marriage contracts dividing material possessions are a French speciality. The two principal contract formulae are *la séparation des biens* (separate possessions) and *la communauté universelle* (all pre- and post-marriage possessions jointly owned). Assuming that no special division (*régime*) has been confirmed by an official contract drawn up by a notary a marriage in France is subject automatically to a standard marriage settlement, the *régime légal actuel* or *régime primaire*. Basically this confirms individual ownership of possessions prior to the marriage and any future legacies, and provides for future joint-ownership of possessions bought during the marriage.

A spouse can dispose of jointly-owned possessions including the family car, but not the family home, and joint bank account cheques do not need to be countersigned. Either spouse is responsible for debts following credit agreements jointly contracted *or* for any credit agreement contracted individually for articles which contribute directly to day-to-day running of the household or to children's education.

Divorces are obtained in the following circumstances:

- by mutual agreement (*consentement mutuel*); if one spouse does not fulfil their marital obligations or acts in a generally unreasonable manner (*faute*);

- or if spouses have not lived together for at least two years.

In cases of mutual agreement, application must be made to a judge through a solicitor – one solicitor (*avocat*) can act for both spouses – and at least six months after the wedding. Since the beginning of 2005 divorces are pronounced immediately as the former three-month 'think-it-over' period no longer applies.

The spouse who asks for a divorce after two years' separation pays all legal charges. Adultery is no longer automatically grounds, a *faute*, for divorce: the judge decides. Not so long ago, up to 1975, adultery was still a misdemeanour.

Maintenance payments for children and spouses (male or female) will depend of course on incomes and, in the case of non-payments, can be deducted by employers directly from salaries. Solicitors negotiate these payments.

PACS

The *PACS* (*Pacte Civil de Solidarité*) is a legal contract in operation since the end of 1999 between two adults living together who can be of the same sex. The main features are provision of mutual support, and responsibility for debts, for each party as with marriages. Joint tax returns can also be made provided that the *PACS* agreement is still in force at least one calendar year after its inception. The closest you can get to being married without being so. There are no 'divorce' complications as the agreement can simply be dissolved without justification provided the decision is notified to the clerk's office where it was originally registered! Married people cannot enter into a *PACS*. The *PACS* agreement goes further than cohabitation (*concubinage*) private agreements certified by town halls as they provide legal as well as administrative status for a couple.

Inheritance

Use of a notary is essential for most inheritance matters – which can be extremely complex. An inheritance tax (*droits de succession*) explanatory leaflet, free of charge, should be available from a notary's *étude* or failing that in a major public library. Editions du Cherche Midi (tel: 01 42 22 71 20) have recently published an inheritance law guide, if your French is up to it, which costs 23€. Independent bilingual consultants, who are usually British, advertise in English language French property magazines. They can be helpful, perhaps after you've first studied or got someone to translate an explanatory leaflet. The notaries' website www.notaires.fr has comprehensive information, but in French only, and very few notaries, who must be French, will be truly bilingual. Free advice from an unqualified person is to be avoided. '*Les conseilleurs ne sont pas les payeurs*' (people ready with advice don't pay the consequences) is the French saying.

French law now allows a surviving spouse to live alone in the marital home they jointly own, or may not own at all, for the rest of their life. A surviving spouse can also now inherit 25 per cent of the deceased spouse's estate or enjoy 100 per cent of its utilisation and/or derived income, under *usufruit* conditions if there are surviving children born from their marriage. The *usufruit* possibility no longer applies if there

La Tour Eiffel, Paris

Typical Metro sign, Paris

Sacré Coeur, Paris

Montmartre, Paris

Champs Elysées, Paris

Montpellier, Languedoc-Roussillon

Fish at market, Vieux Nice

Nice, Cote d'Azur

La Rue Obscure, Villefranche-sur-Mer, French Riviera

Breil-sur-Roya, Alpes-Maritimes

Riquewihr, Alsace

Chenonceau, Loire

are also children surviving from a previous relationship. If there are no surviving children at all the surviving spouse receives 50 per cent of the estate with the other 50 per cent divided equally between the deceased's surviving parents. The surviving spouse receives the entire estate if there are no surviving children or deceased's surviving parents.

Limited donations, when alive, can be made to spouses or children to relieve inheritance tax. Wills can be drawn up by a notary using a *forme internationale* which may correspond best to your particular situation.

Banking, credit agreements and debts

A few of the most important considerations are given below.

International credit/debit cards

Computerised machines used by shops and restaurants authorise, or don't authorise, payments so the transaction is clear and payment guaranteed. Cash withdrawals from banks, using the card as a debit card, debit your account immediately. Used as a limited period of credit card, payments made on or around the eighteenth of the month are debited to your account at the end of the following month giving approximately six weeks' credit. Your bank will penalise you heavily if you have insufficient funds or insufficient overdraft allowance to cover a withdrawal. Some banks now charge your account for cash withdrawals made using another bank's cash-point (*distributeur*). Don't use your card to withdraw small amounts when abroad if the card, for example, is issued in France and you're using it in the UK or another non-euro country. Standard charges are relatively high.

Ingenious hackers can obtain your card details from cash-points. Cover over the keypad when you enter your PIN.

Cheques

Falsified amounts on cheques or fraudulent use of stolen cheques are more commonplace than hackers fraudulently using credit and debit card information, although these operations receive less publicity. A transparent tape for sticking over cheque amounts, which cannot be unstuck without rendering the cheque null and void, prevents cheque amounts being altered.

If you are receiving a cheque for a large payment, a certified bank cheque (*chèque certifié*) guarantees payment provided the cheque is presented within eight days. A cheque drawn by a bank on its own funds (*chèque de banque*) also guarantees payment and is valid much longer, one year and eight days, like cheques drawn on personal accounts.

Writing a post office or bank cheque which bounces has serious repercussions. All remaining cheque forms must be returned to the bank and new cheque books will not be issued until payment of the amount due is made. If payment is not made a ban on writing cheques for five years is enforced and the central Banque de France records this information on their blacklist data bank. This ban does not preclude opening a new bank account.

Cash

Counterfeiters have successfully produced high denomination euro notes. Be particularly wary of notes above 50€. If in doubt, don't accept these notes from shopkeepers (or anyone else for that matter) even though they may have accepted your higher denomination note which was safely obtained from a bank. A shop that accepts a high denomination note will almost certainly have a machine which verifies it, but they may still have a pre-machine counterfeit note.

HP agreements

Consumer law allows a seven-day cooling off period for credit agreement for retail or wholesale, mail order or door-to-door purchases.

Excessive debts (*surendettement*)

Accidents which have not been insured against, unemployment which is difficult to insure against and getting carried away by attractive consumer goods offers can all produce a *surendettement* situation which is officially recognised by special Commissions. The Commissions review the situation following a request from the debtor who sets out their family situation, debts, income and details of their property/possessions. In the majority of instances the Commission's judge manages to revise payment schedules to satisfy both creditors and debtors.

Business debts cannot be included with household debts for the consideration of the *Commission de conciliation.*

Useful vocabulary

aide juridictionnelle	legal aid
avis d'imposition	tax notice
carte de séjour	residence permit
commissariat	national police station
concubinage	cohabitation
congé de maternité	maternity leave
congé parental d'éducation	extended post-natal maternity/paternity leave
conseiller municipal	town councillor
député	MP
droits de succession	inheritance tax
honoraires	fees
huissier	bailiff
police d'assurance	insurance policy
prime	premium
surendettement	excessive debt
usufruit	right of enjoying the use and advantages of another's property

7
Leisure Activities

This is a vast subject and the topics have been chosen using the following criteria:

- Are there better and more opportunities for the activity in France than elsewhere?

- Is the activity one which is particularly followed in France?

- Is it an activity that a non-French person may have never thought of taking up in their own country?

Experienced practitioners should also find some new information to help them to get more out of their activity at a better price.

DIY

Although food purchase accounts for the largest segment of the household budget, spending on DIY (*bricolage*) materials and tools is massive and increasing all the time with more and more people buying their own property. Over 50 per cent of the French have their own property and approximately 25 per cent of executive classes have a second property. It is estimated that around one-third of all these property owners have a renovation or building project in mind. This excludes DIY jobs required to finish off these projects, and day-to-day maintenance and DIY improvements.

If you are buying a property for DIY renovation, remember that nearly all exterior alterations to a property require planning permission (*permis de construire*) or official notification (*déclaration de travaux*) of the work intended, lodged with your town hall at least one month *before* any work can start. The town planning regulations (*Code de l'Urbanisme: CLU*) applicable throughout France, with any supplementary regulations for your particular area, should be consulted at the *Service d'Urbanisme* in the town hall.

DIY interior redecoration saves approximately two-thirds of the cost of using a professional painter and an interior decorator. Up until the end of 2005, however, VAT (*TVA*) at only 5.5 per cent applies to conversion, improvement, fitting, renovation and maintenance work and to most materials supplied and fitted by the *same* professional for residential properties over two years old. This reduced rate – it is otherwise 19.6 per cent – may be continued. Do the sums. Minor work suggests DIY, such as putting up shelves, tiling a wall, painting or wall-papering individual rooms if they don't all have to be done at the same time, assembling small garden sheds on flagstone foundations, building a small barbecue and even laying simple terraces. Putting in new kitchens and bathrooms invites professionals.

Buying DIY products

National chains such as LeRoy Merlin, Castorama and LaPeyre have a tremendous selection of products in their large stores. See Useful Websites. LaPeyre has online ordering in English and both Castorama and LeRoy Merlin have explanatory leaflets (in French) with diagrams covering particular DIY jobs. Look out also for in-store practical lectures/demonstrations and TV video demonstrations on various topics ranging from mixing cement (*préparation en maçonnerie, dosage*) to installing a partition wall (*mettre une cloison en placo*) and swimming pool maintenance (*traitement de l'eau de sa piscine*). LaPeyre have attractively laid out showrooms with comprehensive catalogues on themes such as doors, windows, blinds, stairs and cupboards for inside and outside work, and everything for fitted kitchens and bathrooms. Stock items can be picked up almost immediately, after having been selected and paid for in the showroom, at the adjacent stock room counters as if you were in a UK Argos catalogue showroom. Both LeRoy Merlin and Castorama are hypermarkets with self-service rows of material and checkouts. LaPeyre shopping is a pleasant experience with well-informed staff giving you personal service and advice while LeRoy Merlin and Castorama staff are often juggling between replenishing shelf stock and giving customers their attention.

On a smaller scale, Mr Bricolage, Weldom, Bricomarché, Gedimat and Bricorama have DIY supermarkets throughout France, and general merchandise hypermarkets like Auchan, Carrefour and Géant Casino all have sections with basic tools, fixtures and fittings.

If you have time, it pays to check competitive prices and calculate savings using no-interest payment instalments, pay later schemes, in-store customer card privileges etc. Websites and your letter box publicity bumf also give the latest deals. You are, however, unlikely to find exactly the same manufacturer's tool or appliance with a price tag cheaper in another store which is why the 'we pay the difference in price if you find the identical article cheaper elsewhere' offers are permanent. Stores will usually refund, no questions asked, an item within a short period if you buy the wrong item (or change your mind) provided you keep the checkout ticket and don't open the packaging. Look for details of the refund policy displayed in the store.

DIY details

In the interests of getting on with your neighbours and generally keeping the peace, DIY noise should be kept to the bare minimum. You can receive a hefty fine if you noisily drill holes or hammer in nails between 10 pm and 7 am. Repeated long bouts of noise exceeding 30 decibels in the daytime are also officially frowned upon and in extreme circumstances the mayor can specifically forbid noisy activities in the community at certain times during the day.

Safety measures should not be forgotten. Use face masks and goggles, particularly for sanding down; you never know when you might run across asbestos (see Chapter 4) which must be removed and destroyed by specialists. Non-slip shoes should be worn for outside work and if you're running up and down ladders.

The following vocabulary table will assist you in finding the right section in DIY hypermarkets, which can be daunting if you don't understand the shelf signposting. The table also includes vocabulary for some basic and specialised tools.

Useful vocabulary

aménagement	fitting out materials, shelving
carrelage	tiles
chignole	hand drill
ciseau à bois	chisel

clé	spanner
clé à molette	adjustable spanner
coupe carreaux	tile cutters; cutting blades much longer than the tiles are essential for cutting thin strips
crépi	roughcast
établi pliant	folding work-bench
étau	vice
lime	file
niveau à bulle	spirit level
outillage	tools
outillage à main	hand tools
papier peint	wallpaper
peinture outillage	paintbrushes etc
peinture préparation	undercoats, etc
peinture extérieure	outdoor paints
peinture enduit	paint filler, coatings
peinture de finition	top-coat paints
peinture intérieure	indoor paints
perceuse éléctrique	electric drill
pince	pliers
pistolet à peinture	spray paint gun
ponceuse	sander
quincaillerie	ironmongery
rabot	plane
rangement	cupboards, storage units
revêtement de sol	floor coverings
rideaux	curtains
scie	saw
scie à métaux	hacksaw
stores	blinds
tournevis cruciforme	crosshead screwdriver

Celebrations and events

Local and national celebrations, boot sales, exhibitions and fairs all provide first-class introductions to the French cultural and social scenes. Bargains can also be picked up at boot sales and consumer fairs.

Local and national celebrations

Statues commemorating the dead of two World Wars, Resistance heroes, De Gaulle, the Allied Liberation etc have their annual ceremonies with speeches from the mayor followed by the local brass band playing the Marseillaise. Attendance at least once is a sensible idea if you don't want to live in complete ignorance of the historical importance of them to your community. In the same vein are *Les Journées du Patrimoine* (heritage weekends) which take place once a year throughout Europe in September. Reduced prices or free visits, and in some municipalities free transport (book your seat), are offered to historical monuments, museums, normally closed archives, etc.

Religious celebrations, even if you're not religious, such as the Epiphany (6 January) which is not celebrated officially means Epiphany cakes (*les gateaux des rois*) – round bun or almond pastry variety – at weekends throughout January. Pancake day celebrations are much more limited in duration and less important. Labour day (*Fête du travail*), 1 May; VE day, 8 May; Assumption Day, 15 August; All Saints' Day (*Toussaint*), 1 November; and Armistice Day, 11 November, are public holidays if they fall on weekdays. Ascension Day, always a Thursday and usually in May, is also a public holiday. The crowning glory is France's national day, 14 July, when the red carpet is laid out with full military splendour at the end of the Champs Elysées for a parade and fly-past in front of and over the President and Government: worth watching on TV and also for the presidential interview on the state of the nation afterwards.

Exhibitions

Local art exhibitions organised by the municipality run for several weeks so even if you have missed the opening (see Integration in Chapter 5) you can still enjoy and perhaps buy something. The advantage of the opening, apart from the free food, is that you can meet the artist who is as a rule flattered by foreigners taking an interest in their work.

Markets and fairs

Private car-boot sales and secondhand (*brocante*) markets, commonly known as *marchés aux puces* are a good source for chinaware and books. Private car-boot sales in particular can unearth some interesting English-language books at cheap prices.

The Emmaüs depots, rather like Oxfam shops but much bigger, are the retail outlets for the organisation founded 50 years ago by the priest Abbé Pierre, now one of the most popular men in France. They have an interesting selection of furniture items, chinaware and books. Secondhand sale or return stores like the Troc de L'Ile outlets have more expensive articles as goods are not donated.

If you're clearing out goods yourself, private car-boot sales are only allowed once or twice a year on set days, otherwise you are deemed to be a professional *brocanteur* liable for business registration and charges. Either way you will have to reserve and pay for your pitch (*emplacement*). Whether you're selling goods or seeking bargains, arrive early. Bargains can also be had at the end of the day.

Spring and autumn general consumer fairs in large towns, often labelled as international fairs, *foires internationales*, are particularly useful for foreigners as they have everything you might need for the house, garden and swimming pool, the latest fashion trends, outdoor and leisure activities and equipment conveniently set out for your appraisal over a few hectares. Prices are interesting as stand holders are keen for business to recoup the cost of their stand investment and expenses.

Food stalls offer samples and you can taste wines. Random wine tasting should not be confused with serious induction courses in wine appreciation run by wine specialists (oenologists). These *initiation à l'oenologie* courses run for an afternoon or early evening and cost around 40–50€. Some courses are run in English.

Specialist fairs on home improvement, interior decoration and furniture will be advertised in the local press, and if you live in an important agricultural area there will usually be an annual fair featuring locally grown produce and regional wines. Beware, if you are driving home afterwards, of extremely popular local wine-tasting festivals in the run up to Christmas, with young wines following the autumn grape harvest!

Major fairs in Paris, which are held annually, are the *Salon d'Agriculture*, end of February, and the *Foire de Paris*, end of April.

Gardens and gardening

French television claims that French families spend more on gardening now than the British. The expenditure may well include garden furniture, wooden pergolas and small open tents (*tonnelles*) because better weather gives more opportunities to relax in your garden, apart from cultivating and maintaining it.

If you want a swimming pool, paved surround, some lawn and flower beds and you're looking at on-plan developments and new properties standing on bare plots, approximately 1,000m^2 overall is a good plot size.

Medium-sized private properties with ornamental, geometrically laid out gardens in the best Versailles tradition are rare. So are immaculate green lawns in the best English tradition (*gazon anglais*) in southern areas. If you do want a bit of England in your back garden, and you live in the Mediterranean or south-west areas, lay down an automatic sprinkler system before sowing grass seed or laying turf. You may need to employ a landscape gardener (*paysagiste*). The notion of 'keep off the grass' now only applies to public gardens as opposed to public parks and private gardens, and seed for *gazon rustique* and *gazon sport* producing hard-wearing grass can be bought in garden centres and hypermarkets. Garden watering restrictions are rare, but several *départements* were subject to a watering ban in the summer of 2005.

Most householders manage to mow their own lawns. Professional gardeners are not interested in off-loading mowers for 30 minute stints on private lawns. They will, however, be pleased to trim and spray your fruit trees on a regular basis. If you spray insecticide and pesticide yourself, avoid doing it if it's windy and always wear face masks and goggles. The instructions on the product packets are not always in French and English.

French gardening

As a general rule, gardening possibilities and seasons in the north, north-west and east of France are similar to those in the UK. Winters may be colder and summers usually slightly hotter. The French Alps, Pyrenees and Mediterranean and south-west coasts have their own possibilities. If you are creating a garden in one of the latter areas a visit to one of the nature parks – see Walking in this chapter – will give you an idea as to what grows naturally in your area. You will not of course be allowed to uproot and transplant any plants. Local public parks where gardens have been created and are tended will show you what a good *paysagiste* can do. The French Alps, because of night frosts, produce plants up to three months behind Mediterranean areas which in turn produce plants at least one month ahead of the north, north-west and east of France. Mediterranean home owners with a few olive trees in the garden can have the satisfaction of having their olives pressed and oil extracted by the local *coopérative oléicole*. Take some olives along to the *coopérative* in late autumn (consult the *Yellow Pages* for *huiles et graisses alimentaires – fabrication*) to see if they are suitable before stripping trees bare. Very approximately, 20 kilos produce 1 litre of oil.

Fencing or bordering off your property is very much a French custom. Local regulations will stipulate the maximum heights for solid walls. Low walls can be topped with green grill fencing for winding plants. Branches and plants from your land or balcony which overhang your neighbour's land should be trimmed by you if your neighbour asks you. In extremely dry fire-risk areas the town hall stipulates an area around your house within which overgrown grass must be cut down to stubble. A point to consider if you have a large plot and are creating your own meadow by sowing seed for field grass with various wild flowers (*gazon japonais*), as this grows to a height of around 30 or 40cm. Investment in a *débrouissailleuse* which costs upwards from a few hundred euros is necessary. It is a hand-held mechanically or electrically operated clearer/cutter with a protective cover which goes right into awkward corners. Goggles and face-mask are recommended.

A lot of gardening books published in England will still be relevant. Dorling Kindersley, who publish the Royal Horticultural Society books, have a comprehensive range of gardening books, and some of the RHS titles have been translated and published in France.

A lot of common flowers have identical or similar names in French. Below is a list of other useful vocabulary.

Useful vocabulary

arrosage	watering
abris de jardin	garden sheds
bacs en bois	wooden plant pot holders
caillebotis	duckboards: teak are best and the most expensive
capucine	nasturtium
chèvrefeuille	honeysuckle
cloture	fence
coquelicot	poppy

engrais	fertiliser
fumier	manure
geule-de-loup	snapdragon
glycine	wisteria
graines	seeds
hortensia	hydrangea
lierre	ivy
limaces	slugs
marguerite	daisy
mobilier de jardin	garden furniture
muguet	lily of the valley (sold by everyone, everywhere, on 1 May)
narcisse sauvage	daffodil
œillet	carnation
outils de jardinage	garden tools
pots	(plant) pots
puceron	greenfly
puceron cendré	blackfly
rose-laurier	oleander
terreau	compost
végétaux	plants
vigne vièrge	virginia creeper

Golf

Golf really took off in France in the 1980s. The number of courses tripled to just over 300 in 1989. At the beginning of 2002 there were over 500 courses. It still remains, though, a regular sport for just a small minority, a long way behind tennis which over the last 30 years has become perhaps the most popular competitive sport played by people of all ages.

There are now approximately 300,000 golf club players, of which 30 per cent are women, while the UK boasts some 1.5 million and over 3,000 courses. Many of the UK courses (*parcours*) are of course pitch-and-putt courses, almost unheard of in France where golf course fairways are nearly always full length.

The *Féderation Française de Golf*, 68, rue Anatole, 92300 Levallois Perret has a most informative website, www.ffg.org with golf course locations, description of the links and club facilities. If you are thinking of taking up golf for the first time the Decathlon national chain of sports shops stock a basic set of steel (*acier*) clubs for men comprising a driver, three irons, a wedge and putter for under 100€ and the same type of clubs for women, but with lighter graphite shafts, at around 150€. All are guaranteed for two years. Don't forget to buy a golf cap with a good sun visor. (Not all Decathlon stores display golf equipment.) Specialist golf shops also exist, notably the usgolf mega-stores with stores in Toulouse, Bordeaux, Cannes, Marseille, and two in the Paris area. Visit www.usgolf.fr.

Many lavish golf-courses have been created by foreign investors for the international deluxe tourist market and jet-setters, in the French Alps and on the Côte d'Azur, and annual membership fees to these prestigious courses are astronomical. You can, however, probably find a course and membership formula to suit your pocket if you only play during the week ie not at weekends when most working people want to play. Prices for annual *semainier* (weekdays) membership start around 900€. If you are not resident, but spend time regularly in a holiday home in France, ask the local or regional *Office de Tourisme* for details of short duration season tickets giving you access to a number of golf courses in the area. You can also pay just green fees, on a weekly or daily basis depending on the golf club, if you're an occasional player. Prices may vary depending on the time of the year. Around 30€ for a week's ticket just playing on weekdays and using your own clubs is reasonable.

English is the international language for golfing terms so you won't have to worry about French translations for 'tees', 'greens', 'birdies' etc. You should note, however, that *mini-golf* is crazy golf: nothing to do with pitch and putt. And property descriptions featuring '*golfe*' and not '*golf*' refer to sea gulfs or bays.

Skiing

France has the greatest surface area in Europe of alpine skiing slopes. The French Alps alone, which stretch in a vast crescent from the Franco-Swiss border in Upper Savoy, near Geneva, to the southernmost ski-resort of Isola 2000 in the Alpes Maritimes, about 80 km from Nice, offer more alpine skiing than either Switzerland or Austria.

Eighty per cent of all skiers in France ski in the French Alps. The season there is certainly longer than in the Pyrenees, which are further south, and the ski slopes offer greater variety and higher altitudes than those in the Massif Central area. People living in the South of France have the attractions of both the sea and snow-capped slopes within easy driving distance and often fit in two skiing holidays in the year. Weekend skiing is also possible, even day trips.

With around ten million French adults and schoolchildren skiing at least once a year in France the Ministry of Education staggers the winter half-term and spring fortnight holidays by grouping the 25 regional educational administration *académies* into A, B and C holiday *zones* so that congestion is kept to a minimum. Christmas holidays are always the same for all zones: 18 to 31 December for 2005, plus New Year's Day. Whether you're an experienced skier (*confirmé*) keeping to red and black slopes or a *débutant* gingerly stepping onto green slopes, hoping to progress to blue, it is best to avoid school holiday periods completely if you want some real freedom. You will also get a better deal from hotels and chalet owners offering self-catering weekly packages.

The school holiday periods for winter and spring 2006 are:

- 18 February to 3 March, and 22 April to 9 May: Zone A. Caen, Clermont-Ferrand, Grenoble, Lyon, Montpellier, Nancy-Metz, Nantes, Rennes and Toulouse *academies*;

- 11 to 27 February, and 15 April to 2 May: Zone B. Aix-Marseille, Amiens, Besançon, Dijon, Lille, Limoges, Nice, Orléans-Tours, Poitiers, Reims, Rouen and Strasbourg *academies*;

- 4 to 20 February, and 8 to 24 April: Zone C. Bordeaux, Créteil, Paris and Versailles *academies*.

There is no real age limit for taking up skiing provided you're reasonably fit. Even physically handicapped people who are in general poorly catered for in France have been thought of. There are approximately 1,600 ski clubs in France affiliated to the *Féderation Française de Ski* (www.ffs.fr). Visit the website or consult the *Yellow Pages* to find a local club. Ski clubs welcome beginners and experienced skiers, and club membership will give you attractive deals for holidays and purchase of skiing equipment. If you want to sell your old skiing gear the Decathlon sports stores organise twice a year 'Trocathlon' sales where you can leave your goods on a sale-or-return basis. (The Trocathlon sales also apply to other sports equipment and clothing.)

Whether you join a club or not the national skiing website www.skifrance.fr (not in English, regrettably) has extremely useful information on the state of the snow at resorts, the amenities offered, altitudes, Nordic cross-country skiing (*ski de fond*), indoor/night-time skiing, the latest snowboard facilities, half-pipe skiing etc. Ski instructors have some command of English, but if you're in a predominantly French class instructions will be in French. An essential, more than useful, phrase to understand is *couchez-vous!* – lie down! – if you speed out of control downhill.

Walking

Doctors recommend at least 30 minutes of energetic walking a day. A lot of commuters to Paris probably manage that every day between Métro and main and suburban line stations. Millions of other people don't have that sort of exercise on a daily basis but they do walk for hours over weekends, and perhaps have a long walk during the week if they're retired, by forming unofficial walking groups (*groupes de randonneurs*) or joining a walking association for a nominal fee.

Skiing country is superb for hiking (*randonnées de montagne*) in the summer and autumn and is dotted with mountain huts (*refuges*) designed more for shelter than overnight stops. Certainly, if you're following a mountain trail for the first time which is indicated by white and red stripes, and yellow and red stripes, on rocks and tree-trunks (*sentiers de GR: grande randonnée*) you should be in a group with a hike leader or guide who knows the area. If you're out in the country on a gentle ramble (*petite randonnée: PR*) walks are indicated by yellow stripes.

The French attitude to walking is as an end in itself, not a means to an end or to an intermediate pub for lunch. Countless illustrated guide books are published setting out the best walks in your area with grading symbols indicating difficulty levels and altitude progression over the number of kilometres walked. For example, and exaggerated for effect, 500m alt. over 1 km is almost rock climbing. Start gently and progress slowly if you're new to walking.

You should have at least a tough pair of walking shoes or boots with good ankle support and a light rain-proof windcheater (the weather is unpredictable in mountain areas). Some basic first-aid material is advisable – any official guide should have this with them – and, ideally, someone should have a mobile phone. In the autumn and winter hunting seasons in wooded and open countryside, avoid hunting parties and private hunting ground (*chasse gardée*) areas. There are fatal accidents every year. The precise hunting season dates can vary from *département* to *département*. Contact the Office National de la Chasse in your *département* for dates.

National parks (*parcs nationaux*) and regional nature parks (*parcs naturels régionaux*) are both protected areas where you are free to walk and enjoy the flora and varied bird and mammal wildlife, provided you don't disturb, damage or destroy them. The six national parks are the Cévennes (a UNESCO World Heritage natural site), the Ecrins, the Mercantour, the Port-Cros island, part of the Pyrénées, and the Vanoise. Details of the 42 *parcs régionaux* are found on www.parcs-naturels-regionaux.tm.fr.

Naturism

The Ministry of Sport in France has officially recognised naturism as a leisure time activity since 1956 following the foundation six years earlier of the national federation (*Fédération Française de Naturisme*). Everything you always wanted to know about naturism and where to go can be answered by writing to the federation at 5, rue Regnault, 93500 Pantin, by phoning 01 48 45 59 05 or by leaving a message on 08 92 69 32 82. Website: www.ffn-naturisme.com. There are 160 clubs in France, over 100 nudist holiday centres and well over 100 official and tolerated beaches along the Channel, Atlantic and Mediterranean coasts.

An estimated 1.5 million people practise naturism, of whom around 50 per cent are foreign tourists. The Germans who started it all originally account for about half of the foreigners, with timid Britons only ten per cent, behind Belgium – which is a much smaller country – with approximately 13 per cent.

The largest nudist villages are not surprisingly in the sunnier *départements*: Centre Aphrodite in Aude; Bagheera, Riva Bella, Villata and U'Fura in Corsica; Montalivet, Euronat and Village la Jenny in Gironde; La Genèse and Le Bois de la Sablière in Gard, and the most publicised of all, Cap d'Agde in Hérault. Naturism is a serious affair and you must strip off completely in official naturist areas. Heavy fines, even imprisonment (with your clothes on) are the penalties for non-compliance. Entrance to official nudist beaches is strictly controlled. Barriers are usual and areas are secluded. A far cry, to take an example, from the Brighton nudist beach in the UK which just relies on the lie of the beach and simple signposting!

While topless sunbathing is allowed on non-nudist beaches everywhere, nudism on beaches – even if secluded – which are not naturist beaches, official or tolerated, can incur fines. Cruising police patrol, with binoculars. Stripping right off in the garden is fine if you have a solarium which prevents you being seen by the neighbours. But if you can be seen, and not appreciated by neighbours, there are grounds for breach of the peace.

Too much sunbathing is not healthy and the national syndicate of dermatologists' golden rules include the following:

- wear sunglasses and a hat;

- don't leave babies and young children in direct sunlight;

- avoid sunbathing between 11 am and 4 pm;

- remember that sea and sand reflect sunlight particularly well, and that the sun is stronger the higher your altitude and the further south you are.

Investment in quality sun creams adapted to your type of skin should not be shunned. Think of the money you save on holiday clothes.

Water sports

Pleasure boating

There are approximately 200,000 mooring points managed and rented out by harbour masters' offices in the coastal pleasure ports. Demand for seasonal and permanent mooring always outstrips supply and a certain number of places are always left open for visitors passing through, and for local boating and sailing clubs (*clubs nautiques*).

The greatest concentration is in the Mediterranean headed by the Var *département*, followed by the neighbouring Alpes-Maritimes and Bouches-du-Rhône, and then the Finistère (Britanny), Hérault (Mediterranean), Côtes d'Armor and Morbihan (both Britanny), Charente-Maritime and Loire Atlantique (both Atlantic Ocean), the Pyrénées Orientales (Mediterranean again) and Manche (Lower Normandy). Prices for waterfront properties with private mooring (*anneaux*) in these *départements* have a particular premium.

If you're a complete novice, hire a skipper and a small boat (*bateaux de locations*) for a few hours with a small group of people to spread the cost and see if you have sea legs. Chugging around on a calm lake is no test. You will need to obtain a pilot's licence to skipper any motorised craft, including jet-skis, of 6 hp or above.

Sailing, on the other hand, is also possible on many inland waterways and lakes. Local sailing clubs will start you off in a small sailboat (*dériveur*) and you can buy a 2m long new sailboat from around 1,000€.

If you are thinking about buying a motor boat visit a boat show where boats, motors, bi-lingual advice, nautical publications and ship-chandlers are in one area. The major boat shows (*salons nautiques*) are the Paris International Show in December, Le Grand Pavois ('the big bulwark') at la Rochelle in September, the prestigious Cannes boat show in September and the deluxe Monaco Yacht Show also in September. Fréjus in the Var has a small specialist show in March for inflatable dinghies and transportable craft, and other ports such as Marseille also have their own *salons*.

Useful publications

- *Navicarte* — Fold-up navigational charts covering coastal waters. Sold in any sizeable nautical products outlet.

- *Le Parler Marin* — French-English, English-French sailing terms, with colour illustrations. Back number special, No. 16, published by the sailing magazine *Voiles et Voiliers*, 21 rue de Faubourg Saint-Antoine, 75550 Paris cedex 11.

- *U Ship Catalogue* — Published annually. Everything you need on board, including mandatory equipment on 5 to 24 m length boats, with a French and English index. Visit www.uship.fr for addresses of outlets and order the catalogue.

- *Le Guide Marine* — Brochure published annually by Météo France. Includes radio frequencies for marine weather reports. In French, but with French-English glossary. Look out for it in tourist information offices. Météo-France, Service de prévision marine, 42, avenue Gaspard-Coriolis, 31057 Toulouse cedex. www. meteo.fr/marine

Fishing

Even the most excitable Frenchman can find total relaxation in casting his line and settling down to watch and wait. There is even a political party whose *raison d'être* is nature conservation, hunting and fishing.

Fresh water fishing requires a licence issued by the national association (*AAPPMA*) which groups the 92 *départementale* federations. Check locally where and when you can fish, bearing in mind there may be complete restrictions in national and regional nature parks and fishing seasons vary according to when and where fish breed. For convenience, retailers selling fishing tackle can usually sell you the annual or holiday period licences. An annual licence averages around 25€. Certain freshwater fish, notably trout, salmon and black bass, must be over a certain size or thrown back in the water.

Coastal fishing is allowed any time of the day or night throughout the year provided local port and naval restrictions are respected and fish caught are at least a certain size. Contact the local *Association de Pêche* in the *Yellow Pages* under *Pêche et chasse (pratique de)* for current regulations. Fishing underwater, which must be without the aid of lighting and breathing apparatus, is not allowed between sunset and sunrise and not within 150 metres of fishing boats and buoys indicating fishing nets.

The following lists are by no means exhaustive, but would-be anglers should know that the Atlantic and English Channel offer: bass (*bar*), mackerel (*mackereau*), sole, plaice (*carrelet*), conger eel (*congre*), sea bream (*dorade*), mullet (*mullet*), whiting (*merlans*) and cod (*morues*); and the Mediterranean: sea perch (*loup*), sea bream, rock fish (*poissons de roche*) and tunny (*thon*). Freshwater fish include trout (*truite*), grayling (*ombre*), char fish (*omble*), carp (*carpe*), roach (*gardons*), pike (*brochet*), perch (*perche*), bream (*brème*), barbel (*barbeau*), black bass and gudgeon (*goujon*). Editions Glénat publish an *Atlas Pratique des Parcours de Pêche* for 15€ which shows with maps in colour where and what saltwater and freshwater fish are found.

Useful vocabulary

appats vivants	live bait
canne	rod; make sure you don't buy a lightning conductor
gilet	safari-type waistcoat full of pockets
hameçon	hook

leurre	artificial bait with hook
moulinet	reel
vairon	minnow

Deep-sea diving

Greatly publicised by Commander Cousteau's *Silent World* films in the 1960s, *la plongée sous-marine* is widely practised in the clear, albeit polluted, sea off the Mediterranean and Corsican coasts. The national federation (*Fédération Française d'Études et Sports Sous-Marins: FFESSM*) has its HQ at 24, quai Rive Neuve, 13007 Marseille.

Although *centres* and *écoles de plongéé* (consult your *Yellow Pages*) don't always ask for medical certificates for initiation sessions (*baptème de plongée*), a clean bill of health, with definitely no latent asthma, is advisable. Swimming happily under water without breathing apparatus is no guarantee, in my experience, that you will feel happy with breathing apparatus, diving suits and flippers. However, if you feel confident, sign on for an introductory course. A whole new world can open to you.

Introductory courses, for which you will need a medical certificate, cost between 150 and 250€. They last several days, giving you four or five dives and a completed-satisfactorily certificate. Progress can then be made to group dives with professional guides. Membership of the *FFESSM* will give you reductions for these dives. The Semantic TS company, 39 chemin de la Bugue, 83110 Sanary www.semantic-ts.fr have just started publishing plastic sets of colour 3D charts of Mediterranean deep-sea dives. They cost 20€ .

Make sure from the outset that you understand everything that is being said. Shaking your head later on, when you're underwater, is not one of the 12 signs in the international sign language. It goes (without saying) that you must master them! The 'thumbs up' sign for example does not mean that everything is going swimmingly. It means 'surface!' or 'I'm going to surface!'. *Never dive alone.*

Useful vocabulary

combinaison	diving suit (when buying one check that the thermal protection will be adequate; the longer you dive the greater the protection required)
palmes	flippers
stage d'initiation	introductory course

Swimming, cycling, jogging and *boules*

If energetic walking for 30 minutes a day does not appeal to you, just swimming or cycling for 30 minutes a day are healthy alternatives. Jogging needs to be approached with care and using the right type of footwear according to your ambitions and the running surface; especially if you have had a back problem or if you are now thinking of taking it up after several years of relatively non-existent physical effort.

Swimming

Around 35 per cent of the French coastline is beach and over 250 beaches and inland lakes are officially rated as clean-water swimming areas with attractive environments under the *Pavillon Bleu* European standard which was created by France in 1985. Beaches range from sand and pebble in Britanny to vast dune expanses along the Landes beaches on the Atlantic coast in the Aquitaine region. Look out for the *Pavillon Bleu* flags or search *Pavillon Bleu* on the Internet.

Additionally there are countless rocky creeks to be discovered where you can bathe away from the crowds, but at your own risk. Local knowledge comes into its own. Mediterranean creeks and beaches have no tides so you can leave your clothes safely in the knowledge that they won't float away. If you are bathing inland the rule is to avoid non-designated swimming areas, especially downstream from dams where sluice gates are opened from time to time. There may also be dangerous currents, whirlpools, or submerged plants and roots. Don't forget to gradually immerse yourself if the air temperature is hot and the water relatively cool. Plunging straight in on a boiling day is an invitation to an immersion syncope (*hydrocution*) which can prove fatal.

Bathing areas are surveyed by the municipality's lifeguards (*maîtres nageurs*) in the summer season (June-September). The water temperature is taken and posted up several times a day, and the green (bathing OK), yellow (dangerous) or red (bathing forbidden) flag flies. The violet flag indicates pollution or suspected pollution, and bathing is forbidden. You will be fined if you disregard red and/or violet flags.

There are approximately 4,000 public swimming pools, run privately or by the municipality. School children's swimming sessions, a guaranteed market, mean that the time pools are open to the general public is limited. If you want some serious swimming, when you don't have people asking you to avoid wetting their hair or have to swim around family groups, join a club or find a swimming complex that has a pool with marked out double-width swimming lanes – keep to the right to avoid collisions with on-coming swimmers! – and another pool which is used for general relaxation. Some swimming pools have season tickets based on the time you actually spend swimming and not on the number of times you go for a swim. The former is more flexible and therefore better value. For clubs, consult *Clubs (de natation)* in the *Yellow Pages*. Also visit the national federation site: www.ffnatation.fr.

Over 500,000 homes have their own permanent pools and the number increases by around 50,000 annually. Sliding curved-roof pool covers increase the water temperature in outside pools by about 7°C which means a few extra months' swimming in the year. British coastal water swimmers should manage six months a year swimming in outside pools with these covers. Properties, exclusively used by the owners, with a swimming pool must have pool safety barriers or a rigid cover or water-contact alarm system by the beginning of 2006. Rented properties with swimming pools must already have a security installation and all swimming pools now being built in properties must have a security installation. Quotations for new pools should of course include this.

Cycling

Cycling has come a long way in France since the first cycling club was founded there in 1868. The Englishman James Moore was the winner of the first official race ever in the same year, over 2 kms, in the Paris St Cloud park and in 1880 an Englishman, Starley, brought out the first two-wheeler with a chain propulsion system. In 2004 there were no Englishmen at all among almost 200 *Tour de France* cyclists.

There are two national federations: one for competition cyclists, website www.ffc.fr, and the other for tourism which also includes mountain bikers, website www.ffct.org. In practice the same equipment is required for either: a racing or mountain bike and a cyclist's crash helmet. Even in the tourist class, cycling jerseys *(maillots)*, clinging shorts reinforced in the saddle area and proper shoes are expected. Saddle bags for packed lunches are not considered appropriate as a tourism outing is a circuit of up to 50 or 60 kms over two or three hours where appreciation of the passing countryside is not on the agenda. Real tourism is a two or three day organised expedition with hotel stopovers or a two week touring holiday, on a sturdier bike, with panniers loaded up with camping equipment.

Cycling alone on bicycle lanes (*pistes cyclables*) or just round the corner for some shopping are other alternatives. Self-protection is apparent with many *pistes cyclables* cyclists now wearing protective headgear, but bells to warn pedestrians are rare. Lowest prices for mountain bikes (*vélos tout terrain: VTT*) for use as a roadster and for cross-country jaunts are around 130€ from supermarkets. Serious *VTT* cyclists can pay at least ten times as much for a quality bike.

Boules

Boules is fascinating to watch. It brings together undoubtedly the greatest variety of physical appearances and outfits among players, predominantly men, of all ages. One of the keenest celebrity players is the 87 year-old French singer, Henri Salvador.

You will see players who are fat, thin, agitated, relaxed, unkempt, immaculate, smoking, not smoking, drinking or teetotal. In summer you can see pot-bellied elderly men with cloth caps, dressed in shorts yanked up by braces over colourful T-shirts. Anything goes. It is almost unheard of for just women to play together. The only similarity to British bowls is the basic idea to get the playing balls nearest to the little white ball (*cochonnet*).

What may appear to be a game of chance at first glance is not so. Experts curve and drop their balls (*plomber*) with great accuracy next to the *cochonnet* and disperse opposing team balls with unerring half-volleys (*tirs*).

If you do play and want to keep your French friends try not to win singles matches on 14 July.

Useful vocabulary

casque	crash helmet
hydrocution	immersion syncope
interdiction de baignade	bathing forbidden (usually accompanied by a sign)
maître nageur	life-guard
maillot	cycling jersey or swimming costume
pistes cyclables	bicycle lanes
VTT	mountain bike

Adventure parks

Based on the Tarzan principle of going from tree to tree, or rock face to rock face, without touching the ground, outside adventure parks provide gymnastic exercise and fun for people of all ages. 'From 7 to 77' to translate a French jingle, and even younger if toddlers are individually accompanied.

Suspension footbridges (*passerelles*), trapezes, rope bridges (*sentiers de corde*), gravity pulley slides (*tyroliennes*) and energetic arm-pull ascents of varying difficulties are features of circuits which last from 45 minutes to three hours: children's circuits, green, blue, red and athletes' (*sportifs*) circuits, just like skiing.

Tree circuits are not a problem if you don't have a head for heights, but you should avoid open rock-face circuits. Prices are around 20€ for adults and half that for children and considerably more if you ask for a guide to take you round. The necessary basic instruction is given beforehand and body harnesses with essential snap hook (*mousquetans*) security clips are supplied. You should also be provided with safety helmets. Book to avoid a possible long wait, and turn up in track-suit clothing to give yourself freedom of movement.

8
Holidays

All employees have five weeks' holiday and in certain public administrations, six weeks or more. Although busy bosses of small companies are hard put to find the time to take a holiday, and about a third of all families in France cannot afford to go away on holiday, more and more people go away several times a year. The advent of the reduced working week to 35 hours means that long weekends are possible and extra holiday time can be built up, but not carried forward into the next holiday year, if employees work more than 35 hours in the week.

The long school summer holidays (*les grandes vacances*) are the signal for an abrupt run down in economic activity with factories closing for up to one month and service industries (apart from tourist sectors) working with skeleton staff. Voluntarily staffed associations and clubs, particularly those run by municipalities, close down when the activities and services they offer would in fact be most appreciated by local residents. *A la rentrée!* (in September, the start of the new school year) is the general cry from the beginning of July for consideration of new business propositions.

Politicians are interviewed for their holiday plans. TV newscasters are replaced by their junior colleagues and the former come back beautifully bronzed. The holidays are *news*.

Where and when to go

Working or retired? Short holidays, or one or two weeks? Possibilities and prices vary tremendously.

If you are retired or can choose your holiday periods, skiing (see Chapter 7) is more attractive outside school holidays. If you want guaranteed warm weather and swimming, at off-season prices and without the crowds, head to the Mediterranean in June or the first half of September. If you're looking for international hotels, traffic jams and sophisticated night life head for the Côte d'Azur almost any time of the year. If you're looking for expanses of glorious sandy beaches, the Landes beaches on the Atlantic coast – the largest in Europe – are coming back into favour after two years of bad publicity following shipping oil spills. The Alps offer beautiful uncrowded areas for mountain walks with warm weather from June onwards. But don't go after mid-August when the weather is unsettled. If the weather is not a priority, Britanny remains proudly regional with its traditional folklore, and has spectacular indented coastlines and magnificent seascapes.

If you do have to drive long distances in the peak holiday periods arm yourself with a current example of the *Bison Futé* national road map which indicates in green the alternative routes which are less likely to be full of traffic. When driving look out for the green and yellow, or yellow and black '*Bis*' (alternative) route signs. Explanations and information on the maps are given in French, English and German. Try to avoid the first Saturday in August, when traffic is particularly heavy, and weekends in general throughout July and August.

Residents can enjoy extended weekend package trips at reasonable prices to major European cities, Amsterdam, Brussels, Paris, London etc from main airports; and if you always have a packed suitcase ready and are flexible in your choice of destinations the websites www.fr.lastminute.com and www.degriftour.fr continually offer reductions on flights, hotels and tour packages. *Chèques parkings*, applicable at many airports, reduce long-term car parking fees by about 50 per cent and can be obtained online – subject to availability – or through travel agents when booking a holiday.

Camping and caravanning

France is a veritable paradise for camping, caravanning and camper van sites, and permanent mobile home residential parks.

Annual guides include the Michelin Guide *Camping-Caravaning* and the Motor Presse France annual *Guide Officiel Camping Caravaning*. The latter claims to publish the complete list of all camping sites (*terrains aménagés*) with utility services, restaurants, etc (nearly 9,000), over 1,000 parking areas (*aires naturelles*) for campers and caravanners, and all the 900 farmland addresses. The enormous Agde purpose-built holiday complex, with leisure activities to suit all tastes, has 25 camp sites alone. *Terrains aménagés* are open from Easter to September with coastal sites usually operating a shorter season.

If you haven't booked anywhere beforehand you should be aware that stopping overnight in a car, caravan, or camper van on the roadside, beaches and conservation areas is strictly forbidden. You can, however, camp in an authorised public wood or forest (*forêt domaniale*) if you belong to a camping federation or can show that you have public liability insurance, preferably written in French, covering you for forest fires. There may be temporary *départemenale* restrictions overriding usual permits. Camping sites, like hotels, are graded on a star system and although the NF *Norme Française* label is not mandatory it is gradually being introduced into tourist services as an additional sign of quality and reliability.

While Britons are the largest foreign tourist group in France, the Germans, Belgians and Dutch are the largest groups of foreign campers. Crossing-the-channel costs obviously come into play. Interestingly, Britons possess more caravans than the French, who, in turn, have more camper vans. For British residents in France who like weekend touring and independence a camper van purchase is worth considering. Camper van parking areas with utility services only cost around 10€ a night for a vehicle. Prices for well-equipped secondhand vehicles in good condition with under 100,000 kms, accommodating three to four people, start around 25,000€.

Major exibitions are the Paris, Le Bourget, show at the end of September (details in English on www.salon-vehicules-loisirs.com) and the Lyon Eurexpo show, *Salon Européén du Véhicule de Loisirs*, in mid-October. Both these exhibitions have stands showing the latest mobile homes. Buying or renting a mobile home on a camping site are alternative holiday possibilities.

Useful information

Membership of the *Fédération Française de Camping and Caravaning*, 78 rue de Rivoli, 75004 Paris, gives reductions of up to 30 per cent in 800 associated camping sites. Annual membership in 2004 was 33.50€ for one person and 41.25€ for an adult couple with or without children.

The www.campingfrance.com website gives details of camping sites throughout France. Click on the map for the area that interests you, then scroll down the list of *départements* for a list, with basic information, in French, of camping sites. Click on the sign *Légendes photos* for fuller information, in English, on the particular camping site.

Below is a list of 12 four-star and three three-star camping sites selected by *Le Caravanier* magazine in August 2004 as being amongst the most attractively situated in inland areas of France.

Name	Location	Département
Château des Marais ****	Muides-sur-Loire	Loir et Cher
Domaine des Bans ****	Corcieux	Vosges
Château de Chigy ****	Tazilly	Moselle
Le Val de Bonnai ****	Rougemont/Bonnai	Doubs
La Pergola ****	Marigny	Jura
Le Paradis ****	St. Léon-sur-Vézère	Dordogne
Les Tours ****	St. Amans-des-Cots	Aveyron
Le Lac des Trois Vallées ****	Lectoure	Gers
La Paille basse ****	Souillac	Lot
La Serre ***	Aigues-Vives	Ariège
Le Sagittaire ****	Vinsobres	Drôme
Le Ranc Davaine ****	St. Alban-Auriolles	Ardèche
Le domaine des Fumades ***	Allègre	Gard
Le Carpe Diem ***	Vaison-la-Romaine	Vaucluse
Le camp du Verdon ****	Castellane	Alpes de Haute Provence

Hotels

Regular holidaymakers in France know that hotel accommodation is better value than in the UK. You pay for the space you occupy rather than per person. A classic example at the lower end of the market is the Formule 1 motel chain where all rooms can be occupied by up to three people (a double bed and an overhead single bunk bed are provided). Formule 1 have in fact 'exported' their low-cost bed-and-breakfast hotels to the UK, but UK prices are still approximately 20 per cent higher than those in France.

There are several guides published annually in the UK on *gîtes* and *chambres d'hôte* in France (see Further Reading). The international website www.gaf.tm.fr provides locations and basic details in English, French and four other languages on over 28,000 camping sites, hotels, *gîtes*, *chambres d'hôte*, youth hostels, etc in France.

Cooked breakfasts are found in de luxe hotels offering international cuisine. Continental breakfasts *à volonté* (as much as you can manage, within reason) can be found in other establishments. Many three star and upwards hotel and motel chains have delicious salad bowl counters where you can lunch and dine *à volonté* for around 12€, making up for missed cooked breakfasts.

Hotels are graded as follows, and just under 50 per cent are franchised or group-owned so standards in those hotels are uniform:

- No star. Five rooms or fewer. This category includes many *chambres d'hôte* businesses, some of which have restaurants. No bath/shower or WC in room.

- One star. Twenty per cent of rooms have private bath/shower and WC. Each bedroom has a chair for each occupant.

- Two star. Forty per cent of rooms have private bath/shower. Room telephone and lift for more than four floors. Someone at reception speaks another language, probably English.

- Three star. At least ten rooms, slightly larger than one and two star hotel rooms. Most rooms have own WC. Room telephone and lift for more than two floors. Breakfast provided. English spoken at reception.

- Four star. Larger bedrooms. All have bath/shower and *nearly* all a WC. Restaurant, and lift for more than two floors.

- Four star de luxe. All four star amenities with larger bedrooms and larger reception hall. WC in all rooms and lift to all floors.

Discounted holidays and travel

Gîtes

Gîtes are not necessarily self-catering. Holiday camps (see below) often have *gîte* or chalet accommodation and you can take meals at set times in the camp restaurant. There are over 40,000 *gîtes* businesses throughout France including those for short stays (*étapes*), groups of children, handicapped people and keen anglers. Competition is fierce. Auchan Voyages for example, the travel agency division of the hypermarket group, offered self-catering apartments in Provence for two to three people at just 99€ for the first week of January 2005.

Holiday camps

Villages de vacances sounds much nicer than 'holiday camps' and they are. Not to be confused with British holiday camps they offer three balanced meals a day (chips are only served about once a week), sporting and cultural activities and are set in natural beauty spots. Family oriented, they provide baby sitting, baby care, and supervised activities for young children and adolescents, while active parents are initiated into the pleasures of golf, wind-surfing, white-water sports – anybody who can swim will love rafting – mountain walks, mountain biking etc or do their own local touring.

They are excellent value. The more or less you earn, the more or less you pay and the weekly rates are published in the catalogues. You will be asked to submit a copy of your tax notice (*avis d'imposition*) when you book your holiday. Visit in English website www.vvf-vacances.fr and ask for a catalogue or visit a Thomas Cook travel agent.

Special rail tickets

In the interests of trying to get as many people as possible to get away for a holiday and to travel by rail, French state railways (the SNCF) offer a once-only annual reduction of at least 25 per cent on return journeys of at least 200 kms. The offer applies to all employees, the unemployed and the retired and your immediate family who live with you, with the exception of children over the age of 21, provided you're all doing the same journey together. (You need to justify your situation.) You can even travel first class, but the reduction is on the second class fare. The outward journey must begin in a reduced period (*période bleue*), which is basically not early Monday morning or early evenings on Fridays and Sundays. If at least half the price of the ticket(s) is paid using *chèques vacances* (see further below) your reduction is 50 per cent. *TGV* trains are subject to certain exceptions.

Other fare reduction possibilities for holidays or any other travel include:

- large families with three children or more (*Carte Famille Nombreuse*);

- *Découverte Senior* reduction for people aged 60 and above;

- and *Découverte à Deux, Découverte Séjour, Découverte J30* and *Découverte J8* – groups from two upwards, weekend return, journeys booked for fixed dates between 30 days and two months in advance and eight days and two months in advance, respectively.

In most cases *TGV* trains are subject to certain exclusions and journeys must start in a *période bleue*.

Train + hotel trips with reduced room rates are always on offer. Visit www.voyages-sncf.com or an SNCF boutique in a main station.

Chèques vacances and *comités d'entreprise* prices

Chèques vacances, not the same as *chèques de voyage* (traveller's cheques), are a means of saving in advance for holiday coupons which can be used for travel and accommodation payment. The coupon values are 25 per cent more than the amount saved and since 1999 all employees can *in theory* participate. Works councils (*comités d'entreprise*), which exist in all companies employing at least 50 people, often contribute from their funds, although it is not an obligation. Employers in any company, regardless of size, which opts to subscribe to the scheme must contribute at least 20 per cent. Employees are subject to salary limits so not everyone can *in practice* benefit.

This may be why many *comités d'entreprise* negotiate holiday deals for their members directly, ie not using *chèques vacances*, with camp sites, holiday camps, travel agents etc. The disadvantage is that you meet colleagues on holiday. On the other hand you are not limited to staying in France, which is a *chèque vacance* condition.

Despite widespread use of *chèques vacances* (over 6 million annually), reduced rail tickets, and *comités d'entreprise* offers, and more leisure time, it is estimated that there are still ten million people, 16 per cent of the population, who have never been able to afford a holiday away from home.

A solution which offers greater choice of holiday destinations and a social environment not linked to your employment is negotiation of group holidays directly with tour operators. You need a good organiser, a good circle of contacts you're prepared to holiday with and a minimum number, say 20. Discounts of at least ten per cent are possible and you pay, as with an individually-booked holiday, with a down payment – settling the balance before departure – directly to the tour operator or through your organiser.

Letting and renting

Letting your property

Being a lessor, even for just holiday periods, is subject to strict fiscal regulations. If you let out your principal *or* second residence for more than 12 weeks annually you will have to pay *taxe professionnelle* (local business tax). You will also be considered as a professional landlord if your annual rental income exceeds 23,000€, or more than 50 per cent of your total annual income is rental. Some resident owners of spacious, attractively decorated homes in sunny holiday areas seal off a room with valuables, and let out their home with all mod cons, swimming pool and three or four bedrooms for one or two months, while they treat themselves to extended holidays elsewhere on the proceeds. You don't have to be the proprietor of a palace in St Tropez to do this. One of the leading websites advertising private homes for holiday rents is www.abritel.fr.

Security precautions should not be overlooked. For example, a terrace on top of a steep slope should have a safety barrier and if you have a swimming pool (see Legal Responsibility in Chapter 6 and Swimming in Chapter 7) it must have a surrounding barrier, or rigid cover or water-contact alarm system.

If you've put your holiday or second home in the hands of holiday letting agents for certain periods, to cover running costs and maintenance, make sure they are a reputable company and keep you informed of all lets. Surprise visits in which you find you have not been informed of a let are not unheard of.

Renting a property

Renting any holiday accommodation also requires care.

* *Arrhes* (deposits) are not reimbursed if you cancel, but you will not be asked to pay the balance of the rental amount. You are entitled to claim double the *arrhes* amount if the lessor cancels.

* *Acomptes* (also deposits) are a firm commitment. You are liable for the total balance outstanding if you cancel. If the lessor cancels you are entitled to reimbursement of all your costs and expenses. Make sure you understand the booking contract.

If you reserve through a letting agent the maximum deposit is 25 per cent of the rental amount, including any holding deposit against breakages, which should not exceed 20 per cent of the rental amount; and if you reserve directly with the lessor the deposit amount is fixed by mutual agreement. In the latter case they may ask you to pay the entire rental in advance. Although you can forsake *arrhes* if you are really not happy with what you see when you arrive, personal recommendation beforehand or choosing accommodation which is on the local tourist office's list of vetted accommodation makes more sense.

Exchanging homes

Exchanging homes for holidays is not a recent idea. Homelink have been in existence just over 50 years. Visit www.homelink.org. You can input your search in the country of your choice in English (or French if you wish) and the annual subscription service costs around 120€ from France which can prove to be excellent value if you 'exchange' your modest home in a sought-after area in France for a spacious apartment in New York, a seaside villa in Florida or a beautifully central Parisian apartment etc. This international website also works for you if you reside in the UK or any of nearly 50 other countries. France, being the most popular holiday destination in the world, has the largest selection of exchange homes. Visit also the Web Home Exhange site: www.webhomeexchange.com. It's all in English.

And check your insurance cover (see Legal Responsibility in Chapter 6) for visitors and guests in your home.

Car hire and touring

With around 10,000 km of motorway network and around 30,000 km of main roads (*routes nationales*), touring France by car is an attractive holiday idea out of peak holiday periods. The east side of France, from a line drawn roughly from Paris through Clermont Ferrand to Béziers, has the greatest concentration of motorways, reflecting the traditional popularity of Paris, the French Alps, Provence and the Côte d'Azur as tourist areas. If you are travelling in the Midi-Pyrénées region a drive across the Millau viaduct in the Aveyron *département*, a marvel of civil engineering which opened in 2004, will cost you 6€ in the summer season.

The website: www.quelleroute.com gives the quickest road route between two points, with motorway distances and toll charges and other road distances. Driving times are given for each section of the journey based on keeping up to and within speed limits. Peak traffic periods are not taken into account and you should add on time for rest periods, recommended every two hours, if you are the sole driver. The route is shown in scroll-down form so you can print it out for use by your navigator.

If you plan to tour a region which is a considerable distance from your home, and you don't want to drive before you start touring, you can reserve a hire car through the SNCF when you pay for your train ticket. You pick up your car when you step off the train. With rail travel such good value, and motorway tolls usually adding about another 50 per cent to the amount you spend on fuel, it makes sense. Transporting your own car by train is expensive and is no guarantee against it breaking down later on.

Useful vocabulary

ascenseur	lift
à volonté	unlimited (food) helpings
camping car	camper vans
chèque parking	reduced rate long-term airport car park ticket
forêt domaniale	public forest
grandes vacances	school summer holidays

location	renting
office de tourisme/	tourist information office
syndicat d'initiative	
période bleu	reduced train fares period
rentrée	back to school/work
salle d'eau	shower room
village des vacances	holiday camp

9
Culture

One of the aims of this book is to help readers get to grips with the French way of life and come through that culture shock better, and not worse, for the experience. Even among French people themselves, regional attitudes and temperaments can mean that people who have been married or living together for years (*en ménage*), and who originate from different areas and perhaps completely different backgrounds, still have to make 'cultural' allowances. A rare but interesting situation encountered is that of a husband who addresses his wife using the formal '*vous*' while she addresses him using the familiar '*tu*'.

Culture, in its artistic sense, is regarded with great respect throughout France and there is an invisible barrier between those who are deemed to have some because they are white-collar workers, those who are experts on some cultural subject, those writers and thinkers of all descriptions classed as intellectuals (*intellectuels*) and the separate mass of people classed eternally as *manuels* (manual workers). White-collar self-made men, bosses of small manufacturing companies, no longer actually doing any manual work themselves, will never consider themselves to be a *travailleur* (non-manual worker) *intellectuel*. *Les Journées du Patrimoine*, however, mentioned in Chapter 7, are extremely popular: an annual opportunity for masses of people including '*manuels*' to enjoy some free artistic culture.

Getting the best out of TV

French television has come a long way since the days when it offered hardly any quality comedy and variety shows. The six (if you include *Monte Carlo*) national free channels now offer book programmes, business programmes, cabaret, concerts, current affairs, films, health topics, historical reports, opera, political discussions, news reports, quizzes, sports coverage, talk shows and travel programmes of a high order and are mainly home-grown. *Canal Plus* is the main pay channel, around 30€ monthly on a long-term basis, and brings you the latest good, and bad, films almost as soon as they've come off the big screen. It also has excellent sports events coverage, usually on an exclusive basis, and in *clair* periods (marked CL in schedules) when non-subscribers can also watch there are some excellent satirical news programmes in the best old David Frost tradition. Toddlers and young children are entertained by dubbed American cartoons early in the morning on most free channels, allowing parents to lie in at weekends.

Here is a personal selection from the free channels using at least one of these criteria: does the programme help to improve your French?; does it particularly help you to know and understand more about France and its people?; is the programme reasonably easy to follow for people whose French is improving all the time?; and is the programme, or parts of it, in itself outstanding?

- *The News* at 1 pm and 8 pm on *TF1*, the main private channel, and at the same times on *France 2*, the state channel. The programmes all last about 45 minutes during the week. Compare, when your French improves, the different slants given to the presentations. *TF1* newscasters are almost permanent figures while *France 2* chops and changes, influenced by higher authorities…? The political scene is always major news and political debate programmes are extremely lively. They need a forceful chairman to allow all participants to express their opinions and arguments without being interrupted.

  Regional News at 6.30 pm on *France 3*, the same group as *France 2*.

  The News on the Franco-German *Arte* channel at 7.45 pm.

- *Culture Pub*. Late Sunday evenings on the *M6* channel. Comparative look at advertising and publicity throughout Europe.

- *Envoyé Spécial*. Current affairs filmed reports. Thursday evenings on *France 2*.

- *Le Plus Grand Cabaret du Monde.* Extremely elegant and skilful circus and magic acts: acrobats, jugglers, clowns, contortionists, Houdinis… Saturday evenings on *France 2*.

- *Stade 2.* A round-up of the weekend's sport. *France 2* at 6 pm on Sundays.

- *Cinéma de minuit. France 3*, just after midnight on Sunday evenings. Classic and recent quality films. English-language and other language films are subtitled in French.

- *Arte* evening channel. English-language quality films. Subtitled in French. Around once a week.

- *TMC (Monte Carlo)* on *Channel 4*. American and British detectives TV film series. Not sub-titled. Afternoon and evening.

- *Les Documents Santé.* Saturday afternoon health topic programme on *France 2*.

- *Arte* channel theme evenings on any serious topic. Two or three times a week. Illustrated by a film and/or documentary.

- *Questions Pour un Champion.* Attractively presented daily quiz programme, around 6 pm on *France 3*. Concentrate 100 per cent. The questions are asked rapidly.

- *Des racines et des ailes.* Architectural and historical splendours throughout the world. *France 3*. At least once a month on Wednesday evenings.

- *Campus.* New books and their authors. Most Thursday evenings, late, on *France 2*.

- *Double Je.* About once a month on Thursday evenings, late, on *France 2*. Interviews 'at home' with foreign writers, artists and designers who live in France.

- *Thalassa.* Beautifully filmed maritime programme taking you round the world. *France 3*, every Friday evening.

- *Ushuaia. TF1*. No regular times. Spectacular look at this planet Earth with intrepid participation by the programme's presenter.

- There are also some excellent wild-life and travel programmes on *France 5* in the afternoons – before the *Arte* evening programmes.

Many of these programmes are late evening so familiarise yourself with programming your video recorder (*magnétoscope*). Note that the 2005 budget exempts one million more people from paying for a TV licence (*la redevance audiovisuelle*), principally because it is now levied with the community tax (*taxe d'habitation*) which does not apply to a lot of elderly people with low incomes. People who do qualify should note that they only pay once even if they own more than one property.

Free digital television channels (*TNT: télévision numérique terrestre*) were introduced in parts of Paris, Marseille and Bordeaux, and in Lyon and Toulouse central areas, as well as the towns of Brest, Mantes, Niort, Rennes, Rouen and Vannes in March 2005 and most of France will be able to receive up to 29 channels by the end of this decade. A simple decoder, costing much less than a digital television, can be plugged into non-digital sets and some adjustment of existing TV aerials may be necessary.

Satellite dishes (*paraboles*) and cable television – if your area is connected – enable you, of course, to watch English-language or other language programmes, notably German and Italian. You should check broadcasting regulations that apply to installation of satellite dishes, and also, if you live in a block of flats, the *règlements de copropriété* applying to them as visible 'foreign' objects.

Books and libraries

Multimedia libraries (médiathèques)

Although France does not have a great library tradition, many dynamic communities have now invested in attractive *médiathèques* with separate library sections for general adult books and chidren's books; general reading rooms where you *may* find a quality British newspaper, *The International Herald Tribune* which is published in France or a slightly out-of-date copy of *The New York Times*; a compact disc library, and an exhibition and lecture room. Note that book libraries are *bibliothèques*, and bookshops are *librairies*.

Communities with similar size populations don't necessarily offer the same amenities, and membership fees range from almost non-existent and for life wherever you live (in France) to over 20€ annually if you don't live in the same community. There is no public lending right system for authors in France so borrowing books is usually free, unless you use a private library. If there is a computer room, membership should give you access to the internet.

The French of all ages have a love affair with strip cartoon books (*bandes dessinées*) which are published for both the adult and children's markets, and a good-sized library will have quite distinct separate shelving and reading areas for adults' and children's *bandes dessinées*. Interestingly, *bandes dessinées* are mainly bound in hard covers – buyers collect them – as opposed to large-format novels and biographies which are nearly always bound in soft covers. All foreign readers of Asterix titles in French will recognise the value of *bandes dessinées* for picking up everyday conversation, figures of speech and useful slang. More seriously, Gallimard publish bilingual editions in paperback of American and British classics which are in some libraries.

Accessing books

Not unnaturally, you will find yourself buying more books in English for personal reading than you would have done in the UK where the wide choice available in libraries means you don't have to buy. The *Good Book Guide* international mail-order service has been meeting this demand from English readers abroad for nearly 30 years. Even if you do have a local or regional 'English' bookshop (check under '*librairies*' in the *Yellow Pages*) write to the *Guide* at 23 Bedford Avenue, London WCIB 3AX, Angleterre – if you write from France – for details, or visit www.thegoodbookguide.com.

Community cultural centres may encompass or be adjacent to the local public library. They provide rooms for cultural associations offering everything, for an annual fee, from astronomy and bridge to playing the piano, and Scrabble.

Annual book fairs promoting the latest fiction, biographies and *bandes dessinées,* with authors and illustrators sitting behind a pile of their books signing copies for customers, are widespread in towns and villages.

Getting the best out of the cinema

With approximately 5,000 commercial cinema screens and countless village halls (*salles de fête*) – you pay slightly less in the latter – showing films, France does an effective job in distributing the six or seven new films, not all from France, America and the UK, which come out every week.

In Paris and some other big cities most of the cinemas will show American, British and other foreign-language films with subtitles in French. Otherwise you can see the best and worst of American and British films, dubbed in French, in the major cinema chains such as Pathe, and sub-titled American, British, Italian, Japanese, etc original language films in smaller cinemas (*cinémas d'art et essai*). The latter account for around 20 per cent of commercial cinema screens and in Paris there is an annual municipal subsidy of 700,000 euros for these cinemas. Although you won't be disturbed by the noise of crackling popcorn in *cinemas d'art et essai*, quite a lot of film-goers have the annoying habit of commenting together on the film in between reading the subtitles. Following a government measure, cinemas are now installing electronic devices which neutralise the sound of calls received by mobile phones which have not been switched off.

Ticket prices are somewhat cheaper than in the UK: between 8 and 9€ for the major distributors' cinemas, slightly less for independent cinemas in town centres and large villages, and around 5 or 6€ for village halls and *cinémas d'art et essai*. The centre of Paris is more expensive. Cinema chains and some independent cinemas sell monthly or annual passes or *carnets* of tickets, reducing the entrance unit price, and there are other reductions at certain times, like just before lunchtime or after 6 pm on Sunday evenings when a lot of people are preparing for the new working week. Over 60s are entitled to a reduction on the price of full-tariff tickets. There are one or two cinema 'weekends' every year when purchase of a weekend pass (*carte*) will give you unlimited access to as many films as you can watch in any or several cinemas during this period, at around half the usual ticket price. You may also find cinemas offering discount coupons on hamburger meals in nearby fast-food restaurants and, no connection at all, some *mutuelle* companies (see Living Healthily, Chapter 5) offer discounts on tickets for certain cinemas if you buy tickets from a *mutuelle* office in advance!

The free TV channel companies have an agreement with the cinema industry not to show films on Friday and Saturday evenings. In addition to television coverage of the Cannes Film Festival in May, and to a much smaller extent the Deauville American Film Festival in September and the Dinard British Film Festival in October, there are regular TV announcements and short programmes on the latest films. TV programme magazines also publicise forthcoming films. All this has helped in recent years to increase film production in France and the distribution of a wide range of French and foreign films. People go to the cinema on average three times a year. (In the UK, average cinema attendance per person is 2.5 times a year.)

Pop culture

Despite official campaigns in the 1990s to limit the use of foreign words used on the television and radio by newscasters, sports commentators and *compères*, public usage has won the day. Publicity and advertisements using large English 'headlines' for impact must, however, show the translation in French as a footnote. *Best of (sélections)...* and *Top of the Pops* are the titles of programmes watched by young pop music fans. 'Corners' in football commentary have ousted '*coups de pied au coin*' – the latter phrase had to be created – although '*but!*' and '*hors-jeu*' quite rightly have not been supplanted by 'goal!' and 'offside'. '*Fast-food*' means hamburgers and '*restauration rapide*' usually means a variety of quickly prepared foods which are not hamburgers. '*Snack-bars*' are 'snack bars'. Former contrived snobbism, using English words when French words were quite adequate, has been largely replaced by a range of Americanisms employed by all but the older generations. The English or American slogans on T-shirts have no particular significance for the majority of people wearing them. 'David Beckham' football shirts are another matter.

On the back of this general development, deliberate marketing has not always gained a permanent stronghold. Halloween evenings, which started in the late 1990s with adolescents and the 18 to 25 age group, have almost fizzled out.

Whiz-kid entrepreneurs often give their company, ideas and products an English name, particularly, and quite understandably, in the field of new-technology products. Even in the traditional French field of gastronomy 'food concept' is used to promote the best of French ingredients presented in a novel form.

All this may have something to do with the general drop in literacy standards in the French language that educationalists have noted in recent years, and the new

Education Act (see Chapter 11) is partly designed to give more lesson time for French for pupils who are below an acceptable level, before they reach the minimum school-leaving age. On the other hand, *La Dictée*, the annual televised dictation test for adults and children, is watched and actively participated in (at home) by hundreds of thousands of viewers.

Useful vocabulary

bandes dessinées	comic-strip books
cinémas d'art et essai	avant-garde/experimental cinemas
dessins animés	cartoons
les actualités	the news
magnétoscope	video recorder
manuel	manual worker
médiathèque	multi-media library
parabole	satellite dish
redevance audiovisuelle	TV licence (tax)
salles de fête	village halls
travailleur intellectuel	non-manual worker

10
Education

Great respect and importance is given to education by the French. The national education budget is the largest state budget, around 20 per cent of France's overall budget – considerably more than the defence budget.

Success at the *baccalauréat* examination, roughly equivalent to the English A levels examination but covering a wider range of subjects, is the minimum requirement usually asked for by employers for obtaining salaried employment in non-manual jobs which require no specific training. Academic requirements, and the procedures to be followed for foreigners interested in pursuing university studies and/or obtaining employment in the teaching, legal, architectural etc professions in France, are dealt with in this chapter.

Children of any nationality resident in France must go to a state school (*école publique*), not to be confused with the British fee-paying 'public school', or to a private school (*école privée*) between the ages of 6 and 16. Under exceptional circumstances the chief education officer for the educational area (*inspecteur d'Académie*) will accept home-schooling and will issue a school attendance certificate which, from a practical point of view, ensures continued child allowance payments. Home-schooling is obviously not in the interests of adapting a child to life in France.

State schools

For 100 years all state schools have provided secular education with no provision for teaching religious education, but following the recent education reform bill an option in religious education will now be possible. Since February 2004 ostensible signs and dress proclaiming a pupil's religious beliefs have been forbidden.

Primary schools

Primary school education (*enseignement élémentaire*) begins at the age of six and lasts five years, starting with the *CP* preparatory year, going on to the *CE1* and *CE2* (second and third) years and finishing with the *CM1* and *CM2* (fourth and fifth) years. The school week is 27 hours, covering all the usual school subjects with the emphasis on mastering French and maths and, with the new education reform bill, an official encounter with the Republic by learning the French national anthem *La Marseillaise*, and an introduction to a foreign language which will usually be English. Young English-speaking pupils starting their primary school education in France should manage very well after a few months.

Your child must be registered with your town hall and will normally be assigned to the nearest school to your home, although if you can show why he or she should go to another school in the same municipality, e.g. special assistance for non-French pupils who have two or three years' primary school education in an Anglophone country behind them, you may obtain a favourable decision. Check precisely what documents are required: birth certificates, proof of residence, vaccination certificates... and any translations of these.

The town hall provides primary schools with all class work materials and books while parents provide personal stationery, satchels and sports clothing for their children. There is an annual means-tested allocation (*allocations de rentrée scolaire*) paid to parents to ensure no child is without the minimum equipment required. Hot lunches are available which are nourishing, well-balanced and subsidised – the menus are even published from time to time in the local press! – and poorer families are totally subsidised.

Secondary schools

Your child will be assigned to the secondary school (*collège*) in your area unless you can show the chief education officer for the area why they should study a foreign language or another subject which is not taught locally. Areas which have a particularly high concentration of foreign pupils who have not been to primary school in France, such as the *départements* of Seine-et-Marne, Seine-St-Denis and Val-de-Marne in the Greater Paris area, have special reception classes (*classes d'accueil*) to help these pupils get to grips with the French language. And French pupils, with the increasing importance given to studying English in schools, now often watch American and British films with French sub-titles on video tapes in class.

Homework begins in earnest at secondary school and satchels start to fill up. Pupils now have personal lockers in *collèges* to relieve the daily load which, in the1980s before lockers were widespread, used to be quite staggering. The four school year classes leading up to the *brevet* certificate examination – roughly equivalent to GCSE – are the *6e, 5e, 4e* and *3e*.

Pupils in difficulty with fundamental subjects will receive special attention and adaptable subject time-tables, following the latest educational reforms, rather than having to repeat a school year. The principal objectives of the education reform are to ensure that all pupils leave school with a certificate or recognised skill, are literate in French, have acceptable mathematical ability, basic understanding of a foreign language and know how to use a computer. At the moment 150,000 pupils, ie around 20 per cent of all pupils in the same year, leave school every year below this standard and 80,000 pupils arrive in secondary school unable to count, or read or write in French.

- Although PE, which includes hand-ball, volley ball, swimming, football etc, is part of the curriculum, inter-school competitions do not exist. Well-structured private clubs, which accept players from the age of six, are the rule and any child who is motivated, or whose parents are, has a chance to compete against other clubs.

- Resource and Information Centres (*CDI*) are run by professionally qualified school librarians. Their responsibilities run from organisation, classification and display of all audio-visual and reading material, including allocation of computer time and coordinating themed displays with class teachers, to policing homework classes and study rooms, providing guidance and assistance for research work etc… all particularly useful for foreign pupils.

- Text books are free. The *conseil général* (equivalent to a county council) funds these and also provides funds for computers and laboratory material.

- Hot canteen lunches are subsidised.

- Vending machines for pupils, dispensing sweets and sugary soft drinks, are now officially 'unhealthy' and will no longer be allowed in schools from September 2005.

In the *4e* or *3e* years all pupils must choose a local organisation or business which will welcome them for one week, giving them a glimpse of the realities of the working world. Pupils considered best directed towards trade apprenticeships leave school at 16, to spend 25 per cent of their time in an apprentice training school (*CFA*) for two years. There they continue general studies, spending the other 75 per cent of their time in real employment which is paid on an age-related sliding scale by the employer. The pupil and their parents must first find – and not without difficulty in spite of the tax-relief incentives available to employers under the national social cohesion plan (*Plan National de Cohésion Sociale*) – an employer willing to sign an apprenticeship contract. Around 250 specific trades, from bakers to painters and decorators, have their individual *Certificate d'Aptitude Professionnelle (CAP)* certificates.

The exam system

Although *brevet* students with limited academic ability are increasingly encouraged into apprenticeships or training courses for specific trades, the new education bill is also designed to ensure that the great majority of schoolchildren (80 per cent) going onto a *lycée* succeed in the *baccalauréat* exam, with 50 per cent of these *bacheliers* obtaining a higher education diploma or degree. There are three types of *lycées*:

- general

- technological

- and professional.

The decision as to which type of *lycée* to attend is vital and parents' choices must be officially approved or not by headmasters. The three *lycée* class years (*2e, 1e* and *terminale*) precede the *baccalauréat* examination with the examination in French taken in the *1e* year. *Lycées* provide up to 30 hours a week of class-work and there is considerable homework. France has at least the same number of schoolchildren between the ages of 16 and 18 as the UK, but as it is over twice the size of the UK pupils travelling daily from rural areas to the nearest *lycée* have a long day.

A plan to simplify the somewhat complicated *baccalauréat* system was abandoned at the beginning of 2005 following massive street protests throughout the country by *lycée* pupils. Note, it is still not known if or when the new Education Bill will come into effect following the recent cabinet shuffle. At present, there are three general *baccalauréat* courses of study:

- literary (*L*)

- scientific (*S*)

- and economic and social (*ES*)

and the decision as to which to follow is taken at the end of the *2e* year.

There are eight technological *baccalauréat* courses of study ranging from industrial technology, agricultural technology, laboratory technology to hotel business, cuisine (of course) and management. The decision as to which to follow is taken before entering the *lycée* and at the end of the *2e* year a specialisation choice is made within the course being studied.

The professional *lycées* are mainly attended by *BEP* certificate holders: students who have succeeded at the professional *brevet* examination. *CAP* holders with good passes are also admitted into these *lycées*. There are approximately 70 different *baccalauréat* courses covering manufacturing and service fields, and practical experience (unpaid at present) in companies and businesses accounts for around 16 weeks of these two-year courses.

The *Conseil Régional* (regional administrative authority) funds or subsidises class book purchase and materials.

Private schools

Private schools are either state-aided (*sous contrat*) or completely independent (*hors contrat*). Most private schools follow the Ministry of Education courses up to the *baccalauréat*, unless they are International Schools which are concentrated on the Côte d'Azur offering bilingual instruction and possibly GCE exams for children of expatriates on temporary postings. Religious education may be provided in the Catholic, Jewish, Mohammedan and other faiths as an optional subject.

Two million pupils attend private schools – often on a weekly boarding school basis – as they have a reputation for stricter discipline and better results. Demand outstrips places available. Completely independent cramming schools take students in holiday periods. Fees in French private schools are considerably less than their UK counterparts, although sports facilities may be poor or non-existent.

Note that pupils in a completely independent school who decide to transfer to a state school will have to pass an 'entrance' exam, while pupils in a state-aided school wishing to transfer simply have to present their school reports.

University and higher education

All holders of a *baccalauréat* can enrol at university.

Most *départements* have a university and many students live at home while they study. First year university students who do live away from home are on the priority list for campus accommodation, which is sadly lacking. Approximately 150,000 more university bedrooms are immediately required. The problem of the general lack of accommodation for students is compounded by high rents, particularly in Paris, and a cultural opposition to sharing rooms. 'It pays to share' thinking is, however, gaining ground and in rural areas, within easy reach of a university, accommodation such as converted barns and mobile home units are becoming popular. Property owners with rooms to let to grant-holding students should note that there should be income tax exemptions on these rental incomes if their (the proprietors') annual rental income is below 23,000€ or less than 50 per cent of their total annual income. (Students in British universities taking a degree in French do not have this accommodation problem when they spend a year as an assistant English teacher in a secondary school in France as part of their course. They are allocated free lodgings, and receive subsistence pay.)

Only around 20 per cent of students qualify for grants and up to half of all students, approximations vary, have to take jobs to make ends meet. It is estimated that 100,000 students are on the bread line. Banks offer particularly low interest rates for student loans and the Ministry of Education unveiled a scheme in September 2004 enabling students to buy portable computers as essential study tools, repaying the cost at 1€ a day over three years.

The first two years at university terminate with a general studies examination (*DEUG*) which must be passed before going on to the third year degree examination (*licence*). '*Bac + 2*' on CVs, meaning two years' higher education after the *baccalauréat,* does not necessarily mean that a candidate has a *DEUG.* Master degrees (*maîtrise*) require a minimum of four years' study, ie at least one further year for *licence* holders.

British students in France

British students wishing to study at a French university must first show, by taking a test which is run by the French embassy in February each year, that they will be able to understand courses given in French. It is essential therefore to complete an application form *Dossier de Demande d'Admission Préalable* issued by the cultural section of the French embassy between 15 November and 15 January. A level passes are a minimum requirement for university course acceptance and a written request for an official recognition certificate (*attestations des niveaux d'études*) of certificates/diplomas is recommended. Visit www.enic-naric.net and consult 'France' for full details. It is best to obtain official translations of certificates and diplomas to accompany your enquiry. Once a pass mark has been obtained in the embassy's French test, the university application and test marks are sent, in the first half of March, direct to the first-choice university which will send it on to the second-choice university if the application is not successful. Apply in time for the initial test otherwise you miss the boat for a whole year.

Grandes écoles

Grandes écoles are France's most prestigious higher education establishments. They provide the future *préfets*, public administrators, politicians, top engineers and scientists, and military officers. Entrance to these 'top' schools is via the *concours* (competitive entrance exam) system following two years' intensive preparation in a preparatory school immediately after having obtained top *baccalauréat* results.

State school posts, university posts and the professions

Primary and secondary school teaching posts for all EU members – and French candidates as well – are via the *concours* system. The number of posts is limited, and once obtained are jobs for life. Only candidates with the best results are selected. To sit the *concours* a Bachelor of Education degree, or equivalent, is necessary.

University teaching and research posts can be obtained by PhDs, or equivalent, via *concours*. Applications are sent directly to the *Président* of the university concerned.

Practising doctors, vets, architects, surveyors, chartered accountants etc or would-be professionals with a university degree should address their enquiry, in the first instance, to the appropriate ruling body or the government ministry concerned. Visit www.education.gouv.fr and consult *Recherche d'un emploi – Reconnaissance professionnelle* under *Venir étudier en France* for the list of addresses.

11
Employment

France is almost at the bottom of the league table for the 15 pre-May 2004 members of the European Union, with between nine and ten per cent of the working population unemployed.

Red tape governing business start-ups is still a mine-field for the uninitiated and the paperwork involved in running an existing business is time-consuming, or costly if it is farmed out to accountants (*experts comptables*), even for experienced employers. Forty-eight thousand companies fail every year: one of the highest rates in Europe. Obligatory social security payments made by employers for employees are high, but the benefits are among the best in Europe. (Self-employed people registering their business as a limited company in the UK need private health insurance as they will not be covered by the French health service.)

Employees in French registered companies in fact cost their employers almost twice the amount of their salary cheque. Nett salary, which is not nett of income tax, is approximately 75 per cent of gross salary. Employment contracts tend to over-protect employees, and employers in small to medium-size companies particularly are loath to take on new staff as employment law gives them little flexibility to lay off staff if business drops off. The need for a company to become more competitive in order to stay in business is, however, a valid reason for redundancy.

Work opportunities

Under the *Titre Emploi Entreprise* (*TEE*) system companies such as tourist-trade restaurants and wine-growers which need to take on seasonal workers can offload the time-consuming administrative work of calculating social security contributions to one of three offices in Bordeaux, Lyon or Paris, provided the total number of days worked by any one employee does not exceed 100 in the calendar year. Consult www.letee.fr or phone 0 800 00 83 83.

A recent report, commissioned by the government, recommended a flexible new work contract which would replace the two main types of employment contracts (the *CDD* and *CDI* contracts) for non-seasonal employees and a new two-year contract should be introduced in the autumn of 2005. See Employment Contracts below.

Every year some 300,000 vacancies remain unfilled. Many of these are in the building trade, despite the increased attention that has been given to technical studies in schools in recent years. Illegal immigrants who have the necessary skills are often illegally employed and exploited, without any insurance cover, as they cannot officially be put on company payrolls.

All these factors are behind the difficulties many people encounter in finding stable employment. Left and right-wing governments have successively introduced premium payments and allowances for limited periods to encourage companies to take on new permanent staff. A fundamental revision of regulations and a new approach to motivate the unemployed is really required for long-term positive results and the new social cohesion plan put forward by the Minister of Employment will attempt to tackle the problem. Visit www.travail.gouv.fr/english.

The laws covering paid professional training for salaried employees and the registered unemployed are receiving their first major review since 1971. Full details in French of the new laws, the choices they give employees and employers and the different types of training programmes available are set out under the same website under *la formation professionnelle*.

'France's leading enterprise'

Artisans, craftsmen, shopkeepers, etc registered as *SARL* or *EURL* (one person) limited companies, or as sole traders (*en nom propre*) or cooperatives, are collectively the largest workforce and proudly call themselves, quite justifiably,

France's leading enterprise. They are included in the company groups known as *TPE, PME/PMI: très petites entreprises, petites et moyennes* (average-sized) *enterprises/industries* which usually have no more than ten members of staff. *Sociétés anonymes: SA* companies are larger, with several shareholders, and include national, multi-national and public companies.

Employment guide for Anglophones

A brief guide to areas and opportunities of particular interest to Anglophones follows. Seasonal jobs in the tourist trade, grape picking etc are not included in this survey. The information assumes technical qualifications and/or commercial experience or adaptability plus a good command of French. Major companies with some export turnover all have tri-lingual secretarial posts. There is a regular, but often part-time, demand from language schools for English language teachers of British or American nationality. Teaching English is not a good option for full-time employment. On the other hand it is a good way to earn extra income for retired people already drawing their pension. A recognised TEFL certificate is the minimum qualification usually required.

- **Paris**. Many multinational and national companies have their headquarters there and proportionately there are many more managerial opportunities than elsewhere in France. Approximately six million people work in the Paris and Greater Paris and Ile de France areas, out of a total national workforce of some 26 million. The growth of the high-speed TGV train network means that living in lovely rural spots some distance from major towns and cities which offer employment is now possible.

- **Britanny**. Technological research, although the national research budget is inadequate.

- **Le Havre**. Shipping, forwarding and transport companies in one of the largest ports in Europe.

- **Normandy and Britanny**. Estate agency employment, for which no special qualifications are necessary. However, to set up an estate agency business in France a professional diploma – see www.fnaim.com for correspondence courses – or *baccalauréat* plus two years' salaried experience in an *agence immobilière* is necessary. Otherwise, ten years' salaried experience, or four years with the official executive *cadre* status, in an *agence immobilière* is necessary to create an estate agency business selling or managing properties. To sell and manage properties these salaried periods of experience are required for each activity. Dordogne and inland Provence, particularly the Vaucluse and upper area of the Var *départements*, as well as the Côte d'Azur – although competition is fierce there – are other areas where English-speaking property sales staff are sought after.

- **Greater Toulouse** area (AéroConstellation), with the largest aeronautical industrial estate in Europe. Visit www.aeroconstellation.fr. The A380 Anglo-French-German-Spanish airbus is assembled here.

- Although parts of the **South of France** have an unemployment rate well above the national average and salary rates considerably below the national average – the sun comes at a price – Montpellier and Aix-en-Provence have expanding high-tech industries, and Sophia Antipolis (near Nice) is France's Silicon Valley and the European headquarters of many companies. Marseille's revived port offers, like Le Havre, opportunities in shipping and related businesses.

- **Grenoble**, the capital of the French Alps, is an important industrial and research centre, and is within easy commuting distance of Lyon, the second (Marseille also claims to be second) biggest city in France.

- **Geneva**'s international head offices are easily reached from the Haute Savoie *département* where property is cheaper than in Switzerland.

- The European Parliament in **Strasbourg** has a specific need for highly qualified translators and interpreters.

Useful information

- *L'Express, Le Point* and *Courrier Cadres* weekly magazines carry advertisements for managerial appointments.

- The national employment organisation (*Agence nationale pour l'emploi: ANPE*) website www.anpe.fr has hundreds of thousands of jobs for unskilled and semi-skilled production workers and non-managerial blue collar staff.

- www.apec.fr is the website for the managerial (*cadres*) division of the *ANPE* with employment opportunities throughout France. There is an *APEC* office in most large towns. Proof of contributions made to an approved pension fund for cadres is required for individual *APEC* counselling or guidance.

- www.keljob.com is another useful site for managerial and executive appointments.

You can record your requirements online for automatic email receipt of job details on all these sites.

Statistics claim that only around 25 per cent of employment opportunities are advertised and that many of the best jobs are obtained through knowledge of the changing job market and which companies and people to contact. Prospecting and personal net-work building are hard work, but effective.

CVs and covering letters

There are of course various schools of thought about the best way to present CVs and what they should and should not contain.

A change in career direction with relocation to France at any stage in your working life needs to be clearly, concisely and positively covered, ideally with your personal details, educational and employment background all on one side of an A4 sheet of paper. Some recruiters claim that an unfolded CV sent in an A4 envelope is easier to handle and stands out from the mass.

ID photos if stipulated – make sure they ooze confidence – should be stuck on or computer printed on the top right-hand side of the CV next to date of birth, facing the job title which occupies the place CV used to occupy, with your name and address (and nationality if the application procedure asks for it) and contact details on the top left-hand side.

If you have considerable employment experience list your *compétences* (what you do particularly well) first using four or five double-spaced lines in normal weight typeface before going down to the next highlighted block, *parcours professionnel* (employment history). Work backwards chronologically, ie from the present. Education, professional training and language details should be set out under *formation* at the bottom of the page. The advantage of this lay-out is that you can emphasise or remove information under *competences* according to the position advertised. On the next page is a sample presentation.

Name .... d.o.b ....

Address .... Position applied for ....

.... Photo

....

Tel: ....

Fax: ....

email: ....

Compétences

....

....

....

....

Parcours professionel

En France

Date. Highlight the function, with company name(s) in normal weight type.
Single spacing between the lines.

En Grande Bretagne

Date. Highlight the function, with company name(s) in normal weight type.
Single spacing between the lines.

Formation

Diplôme d'university ....
(or) baccalauréat britannique (subjects)

Formation professionnelle ....

Langue maternelle, **anglaise/italien/allemand** etc.

A *lettre de motivation*, the letter which accompanies the CV, should always be hand-written if an application is being sent through the post. The letter is an integral part of the application, not just a covering letter referring to the appointment concerned. Bear in mind that the *lettre de motivation* has one goal: obtaining an interview. It should not exceed one page and the text should be composed of three similar-length paragraphs:

- 'You' referring to the company advertising the appointment and knowledge of their business activity.

- Followed by 'I' – experience and personal qualities which correspond to details in the advertisement.

- Concluding with 'we', how the candidature should be of interest to the advertiser and, possibly, a mention of one idea for the company which the candidate could put into practice if they were employed.

If salary requirements are asked for in the advertisement, give a salary range which is in line with the market ratings (see Salaries below) and not personal wishes.

Employment contracts

Secondment to a subsidiary or an associated company in France can mean that the employee is still subject to the head office company's social security regime. The first 12 months' health cover is provided by the new European health card (*Carte Européenne d'Assurance Maladie*) which replaces the former E111 and E128 cards. Make sure your company has obtained this health card for you. Payment of premiums for top-up health insurance premiums – see *mutuelles* in Living Healthily, Chapter 5 – is something to be negotiated with the employer. A permanent posting to a French company should be specified in a *contrat à durée indéterminée: CDI*, which is subject to French employment law (*le Code du Travail*).

The two principal contracts at present covering employment obtained in France are the *CDI* and the *contrat à durée déterminée: CDD* (fixed period contract). Both types of contract usually include a trial-period clause which can be exercised by either employer or employee to withdraw from the agreement. The maximum period at present for which a *CDD* with the same employer – other than in the public and civil services for which only French nationals are eligible – can run is 18 months. A *CDI* is necessary afterwards to stay with the same employer. Don't be surprised if *CDI* contracts run to several numbered pages all of which need to be initialled by the employee and the employer before both sign at the foot of the final page. Clauses precluding any immediately subsequent employment with a direct competitor should not be accepted and attention should be paid to clauses in *CDD* contracts which stipulate heavy financial penalties – linked sometimes to turnover generated by the employee – if the employee breaks the contract after any trial period. The employer has a valid case if their customers are extremely local and an ex-employee creates a business almost next door to them (a hairdresser's for example) with identical products or services and poaches their clientele, thus ruining the former employer's business.

The cost of getting to work is quite generously covered by income tax allowances. For example the employee can justify why they must live more than 40 kms away from where they work. There is also a case, but there is no hard and fast law about this, for employers to pay employees, such as secretaries or assistants, for time taken to get to an occasional work location other than the usual place of work when this runs over normal working hours and takes considerably more time than the journey to the usual place of work. This should ideally be written into the employment contract. Obviously this cannot apply to full-time representatives on the road permanently and managerial (*cadres*) staff who are expected to work out of office hours as part of the job, or to roving executives who regularly visit other group offices.

The 35-hour working week, the shortest official working week in the world, is now more flexible than when it was originally introduced for companies with more than 20 staff in 2000 and all other companies in 2002. Employees may now be offered up to an additional 220 hours of work a year by their employees.

All employment contracts with a company in France must be written in French throughout. English words such as 'weekend' have been officially part of the French language, as '*week-end*', for many years. However, English words such as 'top' and 'look' which are used colloquially are not valid for contracts.

Portage-salariale and *groupement des employeurs* services are recent concepts for contracts. They both involve a tripartite system, with an employee working through an administrative organisation that pays their salary and social security charges and invoices the third party company where the employee works on a short or long-term basis. These systems offer flexibility for companies which cannot afford a full-time employee, although they will pay the administrative organisation around ten per cent of the employee's cost. Employees can thus work full time if they find several contracts at the same time.

Employing home help

As a home owner, employment of a home help/cleaner, occasional gardener, etc can be done without a contract, but quite legally, through the *Chèque Emploi Service* system. The number of hours to be worked and the rate are agreed in advance. The person providing the domestic service becomes salaried for that period and is paid by the homeowner using special cheques and preaddressed salary declaration forms available from banks. The 2005 national budget allows the home owner to deduct 50 per cent of the total cost – social security charges and the salary paid – for the year, up to a maximum cost of 15,000€, as a tax-deductible expense against their annual income. The maximum cost for handicapped people (with at least 80 per cent invalidity) is 20,000€. The home concerned must be the administrative domicile: where the income tax form is sent.

Company staff benefits and basic conditions

Apart from the usual hygiene and safety regulations, all companies with at least 25 members of staff are obliged, if requested by staff, to provide an area away from offices and workshops where they can eat lunch. Luncheon vouchers (*titres de restaurants*) are provided by many employers with employees paying between 40 and 50 per cent of the cost.

Companies with over 50 staff must have a works committee (*comité d'entreprise*) which is elected every two years and funded to the tune of 2 per cent of the total salary bill. This allocation can be used to provide free luncheon vouchers. In practice, works committees offer a wide range of financial benefits and price advantages covering accommodation, supplementary health and retirement plans, consumer goods, holidays, cinema, theatre and sports events tickets, excursions, sporting and recreational activities, Christmas presents and staff parties etc.

Salaries

Two million employees, excluding farm workers and temporary workers, are paid the minimum basic wage: the *SMIC*. The amount is revised every year in July and in

2005 it rose by nearly six per cent to 1,217.91€ a month gross for adult employees working the 35-hour week. While it does give thousands of workers a minimum wage they might not otherwise have negotiated it is also used by employers to keep wages for newly employed unskilled workers down to a strict minimum.

Although the *SMIC* gives low-paid workers a better deal than their counterparts in the UK, management level (*cadres*) salaries are slightly less than in the UK. *L'Express* weekly magazine publishes an annual survey of management salaries showing maximum, average and minimum salaries taking into account number of years' experience, company turnover, company size – depending on the position concerned – and showing any perks and performance related bonuses. Visit www.lexpress.fr and consult *l'actualité de l'emploi* and fill in your details to see what you should be earning. Compare this with results from www.infosalaire.fr or Minitel 3617 Infosalaire. Perfect mastery of another language, particularly English, should pay more, providing it is coupled with another foreign language (other than French!).

Jobs may be advertised with annual salary amounts or a remuneration bracket composed of basic salary plus a variable figure, but employment contracts often specify the monthly equivalents. Keep all salary slips. They may need to be produced for retirement pension applications when the time comes.

Redundancy

There is a set procedure which employers must follow. This can vary, giving additional compensation and retraining opportunities for employees, depending on the collective agreement (*convention collective*) for the type of employment. Earning better profits is not a valid reason for making employee(s) redundant, but ensuring a company's survival by remaining competitive in the marketplace is.

The procedure that applies to a company with fewer than 50 employees, ie without a *comité d'entreprise*, is an initial instruction to attend an explanatory interview when the possibility of redundancy is mooted and any other possible employment opportunities within the company are discussed. The employee can be accompanied by the staff member who represents the staff's interests (*délégué du personnel)* or, failing this, can choose to be accompanied by an official from a locally appointed 'redundancy' panel. If redundancy is the employer's only solution they must confirm this by registered letter to the employee. The obligatory period of paid notice can be worked, or not worked, at the employer's discretion. Two hours a day paid time is allowed for prospecting for new employment.

The management of companies with at least 50 employees, and which plan to make at least ten employees redundant, must consider solutions such as regrading, redeployment, outplacement, retraining, reduction of the working week etc put forward by the *comité d'entreprise*. In companies with over 1,000 employees there is a paid period of organised counselling and training (*congé de reclassement*) lasting from four to nine months. In practice, this applies to several employees when there are massive lay-offs.

The amount of redundancy payment depends on the number of years the employee has been continuously employed by the same company with a *CDI* contract and also on the *convention collective*. The local *Direction Départementale du Travail* office can confirm entitlement. All employees have priority in the first 12 months after the end of their employment for any new job opportunity for which they are eligible in their former company.

Useful vocabulary

ANPE	national employment organisation
APEC	national employment organisation for executives
Carte Européenne d'Assurance Maladie	European health card
CDD	fixed period employment contract
CDI	permanent employment contract
comité d'entreprise	works committee
convention collective	collective (trade) agreement
délégué du personnel	staff representative
expert comptable	qualified accountant
groupement des employeurs	employers' association for salaried contract staff
portage salariale	flexible method of employing salaried staff
titres de restaurant	luncheon vouchers

12
Dealing with Bureaucracy and Businesses

Bureaucracy

The internet means that you can complete your tax return online if you've left it up to the last moment and send it straight to the Income Tax office (*hôtel des impôts*). The internet has also made social security 70 per cent repayments for visits to GPs much quicker by using the *Vitale* health card – see Living Healthily, Chapter 5. However, the internal cogs of many government departments still grind along slowly and systems are still complicated. The 35-hour week has not helped. Budgets are tight so that new staff cannot necessarily be taken on, even on a temporary basis.

Officialdom is aware of the problem. Waiting rooms in many official buildings are now more attractive with comfortable seating, drinks vending machines and clearly indicated ticket number dispensing machines with 'next number' illuminated signs to make sure you don't miss your turn! Depending on the enquiry, appointments can be made and there is usually a receptionist who will give your enquiry and paper work a preliminary scan to see if you need to see anyone else or if you have everything you need. There is now a national phone assistance service number, 3939. For the price of a local call (8 am–7 pm weekdays and 9 am–2 pm Saturdays) you can ask for guidance in getting all the paperwork right for your enquiry before you even leave home, and also on the right government or official department to contact. This is a citizen's information service. The free three-way calling service (*conversation à trois*) operated by France Telecom is most helpful if you need help with your French when you phone. Visit www.francetelecom.com then click successively on *agence sur le net, votre ligne, les services* followed by *mes services* and *les services compris* for instructions to register your phone line for this service.

If your enquiry requires you to produce certified photocopies of original documents, don't rush to a notary's office to get them to witness your photocopying. The local town hall will stamp your copies '*photocopies conformes*', free of charge, provided they see the originals at the same time. Translation by a certified translator (*traducteur assermenté*) of English documents (birth, death, marriage, divorce certificates, etc) may also be necessary for official purposes and the British Embassy or Consulate office have lists of these translators. The translation fees are laid down and are not negotiable.

Getting it right

Correctly lodging your application or enquiry is half the battle. For example, application for property conversions, extensions or new building projects which result in a habitable floor surface area of over 170 m^2 must be accompanied by an architect's plans and four copies of the *permis de construire* completed application form.

Delivering applications or making enquiries in person gives you the opportunity to establish some sort of relationship with someone, which you can politely use later on if you wish to know what progress is being made.

'Standard' applications like a request for planning permission have standard consideration periods. There is no point in chasing a planning permission application before at least two months are up. While most people agree that the 35-hour week is the last thing that French bureaucracy required, Wednesdays can be a good day for getting through on the phone to the head of a department (*chef de service*) as a lot of (junior) mothers are off work looking after their children during the mid-week school break.

Writing official letters

You will inevitably occasionally need to write a letter to a bureaucratic department (town hall, social security office, income tax office, pensions office). Don't be surprised when you do get a reply if it's not signed. The date, letter reference and department's stamp suffice. The reply may also take some time as advice, information or a commitment in a letter is officialdom's last resort. When filling in forms put a cross in a box and not a tick to confirm information or choice.

Your letter should ideally be addressed for the attention of the person you are certain is at that time dealing with your *dossier* (file), or failing that the *chef de service* – even if you don't know their name, or are pretty certain that their incoming mail will be filtered and perhaps dealt with by someone else. The address of the organisation or company – this applies to all correspondence – preceded by the name or title of the person to whom you are writing should be on the top right-hand side of the letter with your name and address on the top left-hand side. The town you are writing from should precede the date. Calendar months are never written with an initial capital letter and it is standard practice to put the address you would like the letter returned to, in the event of it having to be returned by *La Poste* as 'destination not found', on the back of the envelope.

Titles must be respected:

- *Monsieur* (or *Madame*) *le Maire, Monsieur le Préfet, Monsieur le Directeur,* when writing to a company manager whom you don't know, or just *Monsieur*, but never *Cher Monsieur*, if the person is not a dignitary or has no special status.

- *Mon Père* for priests or *Monsieur le Curé* if you're an atheist! *Monseigneur* is used for cardinals and bishops.

- Military officers: *Mon Général* etc.

Endings should be formal and correspond to yours faithfully or yours sincerely:

- *Je vous prie de croire, Monsieur/Madame/Mon etc ...* (the surname or title) *à l'assurance de mes salutations distinguées.*

- A man writing to a *Mademoiselle* can use the ending: *Veuillez agréer, Mademoiselle etc..., l'expression de mes sentiments les meilleurs.*

Businesses

Dealing with private businesses (manufacturers, shops, service companies, etc) as a customer requires some care.

- In a self-service supermarket, hypermarket, cafeteria or petrol station no special skills are involved. There is no negotiation. Promotional prices displayed in-store are, however, not always recorded at check-outs so check your bill as it is being printed out.

Wholesale electrical appliance stores, which are often open to the general public on application for a special card (*carte privilège*), and cash-and-carry outlets like Métro which are open to professional or business people who qualify as trade customers, usually show prices '*HT*': exclusive of VAT. Value added tax (*TVA*) is 19.6 per cent on electrical goods so make sure you are getting a good buy if you can shop in either of these outlets.

Unsolicited mail-order offers are tempting. Check carefully that you have understood all the small print and keep a copy of the coupon you have sent off for your free gift. Consumer protection disappears after the initial seven-day cooling off period expires (see HP Agreements in Chapter 6).

- Always spell or better still write out your name in travel agents when ordering airline tickets. 'G/g' is pronounced as a soft 'jay', 'J/j' as a soft 'gee' and 'I/i' as 'e'. Although up to three spelling mistakes, apparently, are permitted in a name on a plane ticket, 'Jean Phelz' instead of 'John Fells' won't do.

- Fitted kitchen stores in particular always have discount offers and extra discounts will be piled on by salesmen if they feel they have a punter. Be wary of the quality and the fitting service if the brand name is new to you (see Estimates below). On the other hand, genuine discounts can sometimes be negotiated on large furniture items such as settee suites in large stores which have daily sales targets. Make sure the item is what you really want. If the store has not been seen to be busy, popping back before closing time having previously discussed the item with the same salesman can be effective.

- Estimates, even hand-written ones for small jobs around the house where you don't really need to compare prices, should make quite clear what is to be done and when, the material to be supplied and who is paying for what, maximum cost, the guarantee period and payment terms. As a foreigner you can always justify being over-meticulous as you need to make sure there is no misunderstanding.

- For major building work (extensions, room conversions, permanent swimming pools…), new fitted kitchens and bathrooms, three estimates are recommended for sensible comparison and evaluation of the going rate for your particular project. Try to obtain free estimates, marked *'gratuit'*. The *Lapeyre* company, a first class supplier and installer of fittings and fixtures for the home, charges 50€ for any firm estimate following a visit to your home to measure up, but this is deducted from their invoice if you accept their estimate. You can of course obtain a guesstimate for products and installation charges in their stores.

If you are promoting yourself or your company's products or services you may encounter problems in getting firm appointments; dealing with the secretarial barrier which surrounds *Monsieur le Directeur*; and getting written confirmation, or even acknowledgements, of anything before a firm commitment is made. Emails following meetings are dealt with promptly, as a rule, but unsolicited fax enquiries or progress chasers by fax tend to be ignored. Programming the acknowledgement-request option on your computer for emails makes sense.

Organising appointments

Two methods have a good success rate.

1 An initial letter which briefly presents your company/product or project in terms of advantages (cost savings, flexibility, etc) for the company to whom you are writing. Their interest ('you' in the letter) followed by your company's or your personal background and how together 'we' could collaborate on a development you know will interest them. This requires some research and, ideally, the name of the company manager or head of department.

   Prior phoning to ask for the name of the person concerned is a last resort. The letter should conclude with the announcement that you will contact the addressee in the next few days for an appointment.

2 Phone and give your name – pronounce it slowly or spell it out – and ask to be put through to the person concerned. If you don't sound French and have a distinctly Anglo-Saxon name you are at an advantage. Then, if and when you are put through, outline why you are phoning and ask for an appointment.

Following up initial-approach letters

This is when you may encounter the secretarial barrier, put up by a receptionist/general secretary or a high-powered management secretary (*sécretaire de direction*), depending on the size of the company. You should explain clearly to whoever picks up the phone who you are and that you are phoning following the letter sent to *Monsieur* or *Madame...* on... With small companies, try phoning just after normal office hours as you may well get through direct to the person you want. Executives in small companies are either worked off their feet or like to make out they are. Monday mornings and Friday afternoons are 'he or she's in a meeting' times and should be avoided.

If you still can't get past the secretarial barrier or the person is not available ask for a date and time when you can call back.

Business-to-business cold calls

This is not as dreadful and as cavalier as it sounds. Depending on where you are in France, you may be able to see the manager directly without an appointment or, of course, you can make an appointment – preferably for the same day. Let them see that you have noted in it in your diary. Foreigners are usually well received. If you have some eye-catching sales material with you this helps.

Firm appointments

Don't be surprised if appointments with small-medium size companies (*petites et moyennes entreprises et industries: PME/PMI*) whose business activities are local are not kept to punctually, or perhaps not at all. Some managers are hands-on and don't have the staff to delegate visits to important customers. Mediterranean France has a poor appointment-keeping record, more a problem of poor time management and a dash of Latin spontaneity than deliberately being impolite. If you have booked an appointment, avoid making it too far ahead as it can be cancelled. It can also be cancelled if you phone up to reconfirm it. So don't. Appointments for visits involving a long journey should of course be confirmed in advance, especially if you're travelling from the north to the south. A quick exchange of emails is a convenient way to do this. Don't expect to be offered a cup of coffee if you arrive early, although this Anglo-Saxon courtesy is slowly gaining ground.

Dealing with works committees can be comparatively straightforward, and involve big business. The decision may have to await the next month's meeting unless you have involved the managing director (*directeur général*) earlier on and they convene an extra-ordinary meeting. Works committees' elected members have set times for receiving commercial presentations for their members. The purchase decision may also be voted for from the forthcoming budget if all funds, including contingency reserves, have been spent. Full documentation will be required, including a specimen contract if you offer a regular service. A retrospective commission paid into the committee's funds can be part of the deal if consumable products are concerned.

13
Eating Out

A 2004 national survey of 3,000 people confirmed that people in the north tend to eat heavier meat and potato dishes at home than southerners, who are much more used to cooking lighter fish and vegetable dishes. Sauerkraut with meat and potatoes (*choucroute*), for example, is standard fare in Alsace, but in the south is bought ready cooked from hot food counters in supermarkets as a speciality dish in the autumn and winter, a halfway compromise with eating out.

Self-service restaurants

Eating out does not have to be a special occasion, as is shown by fast-moving lunchtime queues of working and retired people at self-service restaurants throughout France. Many retired couples lunch out several times a week in Flunch or Casino *caféterias*. There are about 400 of these restaurants throughout France and an excellent three-course meal can be had for about 10 euros a head. (Casino publish a free road map of France, available in their restaurants, pinpointing their outlets and with directions on how to drive to them.) Small starter salads – you pick and mix your selection – cost 2–3€, grills (to order) or main meat or fish dishes up to around 6€, and tarts, fruit or delicious ice-cream concoctions – the latter are particularly good value – up to 3€. Flunch offer unlimited servings of a healthy selection of seven vegetables. You are of course only given one plate per person! Self-service restaurants have timeless, standard, not unpleasant décors which haven't changed much since their inception over 30 years ago, with picture windows all round outside

154

walls and Smoking and Non-smoking sections. Buffalo Grill steak houses are popular for lunches and dinners and service is quick, the décor cosy, quality consistent and prices reasonable. Motorway self-service restaurant standards vary, but choice of food is much more limited and prices considerably more than self-service meals in towns and shopping centres. A two course self-service motorway meal will cost about the price of a three course self-service meal off the motorway.

Large towns will have at least one self-service South-East Asian restaurant, usually Vietnamese. Complete take-away meals are not as popular as in the UK, but take-away starters such as spring or pancake rolls are. Old take-away habits die hard. American tourists have been known to ask where they can get a good traditional hamburger which they can eat hurrying about from place to place while pizza kiosks and baguette sandwich stands everywhere offer wider choice and the same convenience.

New types of restaurants

Paris, in particular, in recent years has seen the opening of new theme restaurants, such as fresh-soup kitchens and salad bars or attractive lunch-time diners where you can have a sustaining, but light, meal for under 10 euros.

Bars and cafés

All traditional bars have espresso coffee machines, and the Macdonald and Quick fast-food chains now offer espresso coffee instead of the former instant black coffee machines. You may still only have instant coffee in some snack bars, or the choice of instant or espresso in self-service snacks at airports. Town centre bars may charge slightly more for coffee served on an outside terrace.

Local and village bars (*bars de quartier*) normally charge the same price if you want to get away from noisy card games and zinc counter political debates or just enjoy watching the traffic and passers by. *Café crème* served in a large cup costs around twice the price of an espresso which only costs between 1€20 and 2€ – compare that to much higher UK prices – unless you're on the Champs Elysées or on the port at Saint Tropez where it costs much more.

Hard-boiled eggs in egg holders on bar counters provide instant mid-morning snacks.

Ice-cream parlours, sophisticated cocktail bars with a resident pianist or 1920s décor *salons de thé* serve a tremendous selection of beautifully presented ice-cream, sorbet and fruit dishes in large glass cups or knickerbocker glory glasses, accompanied by Chantilly cream and with or without alcohol. But don't expect the same prices as ice-cream concoctions in self-service restaurants.

Wine bars of course don't exist as such. The Gallic response is beer bars, serving high-alcohol-content bottled beer from all over the world. British style pubs, apart from in Paris, are rare, but Irish bars with bottled Guinness are found in most large towns. Often situated near mainline stations or town squares, an Irish bar in France is not the best venue for a quiet drink before or after an international football match with supporters from northern Europe. One of the most famous cocktail bars in Paris is Harry's American Bar, 5 rue Daunou. The bloody Mary and sidecar cocktails were created here.

Bistros and brasseries

Lunches in bistros and *brasseries* away from exclusive areas in the height of the tourist season are good value, with a chef's special every day. Small villages where the only bar is also the only restaurant are excellent value and often have a speciality on the menu using local produce (*produits de terroir*). As a lot of the clientele throughout the year is the local population they have an interest in providing good food.

Bistros in larger villages and towns only serving meals, as opposed to *brasseries* whose trade are drinks and meals, can be found serving a choice of first-class three course set meals, beautifully presented in attractive décor with competent service, for around 15€, excluding wine and coffee.

The federation of bar proprietors is beginning to institute its own rating system with a *label* for service, food and amenities. Restaurant proprietors continually lobby the government to reduce the VAT rate on meals from 19.6 per cent to 5.5 per cent and are making some progress. A lot of medium grade restaurants need to increase their profits slightly without increasing meal prices, if they want to stay in business. The cost of additional staff or overtime payments due to the reduced 35-hour working week and falling turnover, with people ordering less wine with their meals, has to be made up.

Restaurant categories

The three-star rating in the annual *Guide Michelin* remains the height of culinary recognition. Establishments' reputations have been made and occasionally suffered severe setbacks through the award and subsequent loss of a star. An immensely popular comedy film was made in France in the 1960s with an incognito Michelin restaurant inspector as the main character. In reality, the guide's rating is taken very seriously by head chefs and restaurant proprietors. A celebrated restaurateur's suicide in 2004 was partly attributed by his family to a down-grading by Michelin.

Service, setting and comfortable amenities are also important. Certainly, if you are touring an area for the first and perhaps only time, an impressive view from a terrace will enhance the enjoyment of your meal unless you opt for the intimacy of restaurants with period 'dungeon' dining cubby holes. Double-glazing to combat howling winds in exposed countryside, adequate sun shades, silent air-conditioning etc are also factors.

It is difficult to draw a distinction between *haute cuisine*, high quality dining, and gastronomic *cuisine*. Prices are the best indicator with highest prices equalling '*haute*'. Presentation, tableware, service, décor and of course creative light cuisine are all features. *Nouvelle cuisine* is still influential, but dining well should mean satisfying quantity as well as quality. If you do notice important price differences between certain menus which at first glance appear identical it is certainly because the quality and freshness of products used are not the same. Restaurants which change their menus several times throughout the year indicate that this is to make the most of seasonal products, ie those which have the best flavour at that time of the year.

It may be possible to negotiate free meals – in advance – against the translation of menu cards into English. Count the number of French words translated. The current translation rate is about 0.08€ per word.

Eating in good fish restaurants will naturally be more expensive than meat and grill counterparts, although you will certainly be able to find a quite acceptable fish restaurant at a price for all pockets in any large fishing port from Dieppe to Toulon.

Foreign restaurants

Vietnamese restaurants, which frequently also have similar Chinese dishes, are the most widespread exotic restaurants. As in the UK, set lunch menus are available at low prices. Indian and Pakistani restaurants are more rare and more expensive. North African Arab restaurants with couscous, the Algerian and Tunisian stew, and tajine, a similar Moroccan dish, are good value. If you like curries you will like these milder dishes, but beware of any chilli sauce as a condiment unless you have a cast-iron palate! Arab sweet-meats, usually an accompaniment to afternoon tea, are mouth-watering.

The Belgian speciality of mussels and chips (*moules-frites*), with the mussels cooked in a choice of sauces, is often overlooked as a tasty filling dish and particularly good value. If you are shopping in an IKEA furniture store try one of their Swedish specialities in the self-service restaurant. A main dish costs around 5€.

Booking in time

National holidays are always a good reason to eat out and good restaurants need to be booked at least a few days in advance. New Year's Eve, the Saint Sylvestre feast day, should be booked well in advance. Special prices, doubling or tripling usual set menu prices, will be applied to cover gargantuan meals, possibly with some entertainment and certainly with dance music, preceded by an elaborate aperitif, continuing with almost unlimited house wine and finishing with Champagne, paper hats and streamers. Christmas Day and New Year Day restaurant lunches are also elaborate meals with several courses and should be booked in advance.

Regional specialities

You don't have to live in Brittany to enjoy the best pancakes. This principle can be applied to many regional dishes, especially if you know that the chef originates from the region concerned. Fresh local produce such as game and fish (*produits du terroir* and *produits de la mer*) used in regional specialities are, however, exceptions. It's best to enjoy them in restaurants in their regions of origin. The brief guide below to regional dishes is merely an introduction. Some dishes which are often overlooked have been included.

Alsace and Lorraine

This region combines sophisticated French cuisine with rural, down-to-earth Germanic dishes.

Choucroute (sauerkraut with pork-based meats) and apple strudels will be appreciated by hearty eaters. Quiche Lorraine can be served with *choucroute* and the latter is one of the few French meals where beer, and not wine, is the recommended accompanying drink.

Fresh-water fish include perch, eel and pike.

Bordeaux area and Dordogne

No stranger to many British residents and holidaymakers, Bordeaux vineyards vie with those of Burgundy as those producing the best wines in France. Onion soups (*tourins*) and truffle sauces from Périgord, lamb from Pauillac and traditional stuffed goose neck are just a few of the region's delicacies. Shad (*alose*), salmon, lamprey and specially bred sturgeon offer a variety of fish dishes.

Brittany

Crêperies spread Britanny's recipes and other creations throughout France. Lengthy menu cards – almost works of art in themselves – in some restaurants have over 100 fillings for savoury main course pancakes and/or sweet dessert pancakes. Brittany coast shell-fish (lobsters, oysters etc) are prepared to local recipes.

Burgundy

The classic *boeuf à la bourgignonne* in flaky pastry – beef cooked in red wine with mushrooms, onions, chopped up bacon – with Dijon mustard is not only for lovers of steak pies. Snails in a variety of sauces are also a Burgundy tradition. Ask for advice on accompanying wines.

The Loire Valley

The region extends from Chartres in the north through the Châteaux country, taking in the Anjou area, to the Vendée *département* on the Atlantic coast bordering Britanny. Game and poultry are plentiful as the area has extensive hunting land, especially around Orléans. *Hachis parmentier de pintade* is a sort of guinea-fowl shepherd's pie. *Poulet en barbouille* is a Berry area speciality: chicken in a rich sauce. Pork is popular in the Tours area and *quiche Tourangelle* is made from potted pork. Trout, eel and salmon are some of the many fish found in the Loire, the longest river in France.

Lyon

The city of Lyon is recognised as the gastronomic capital of France. One of the most common historical explanations forwarded for this is that the confluence of the Rhône and Saône rivers provided a strategic trading point for animal fodder and, as a side-effect, the establishment of first-class eating houses for the traders.

Today, with rapid communications from Paris, Marseille or elsewhere, travellers to Lyon for the day can enjoy a first-class lunch as part of their day's programme. *Pochouse*, an assortment of fresh-water fish stewed in white wine, is an excellent fish meal and Bresse chicken, in all its cooked forms, is a guarantee of quality. The great majority of frogs-legs consumed in France come from the Lyons area. Make sure you are being offered the genuine local article as demand outstrips supply!

The Dauphinois and Savoy areas

Linked to the Lyon areas gastronomically and geographically, both areas have their specialities.

Potato and cheese crusted pie (*gratin dauphinois*) and the crayfish tail in a sauce dish (*gratin de queues d'écrivisses*) are the old Dauphine province's classics. The Savoy Alps, apart from fondues, have fine sliced cooked hams and *tartiflette*, a hot savoury flan topped with sliced potato, cream, chopped onion and strips of smoked ham. Freshwater fish include carp and burbot.

The Mediterranean coast and Provence

Taken here as one area, the variety of salad, fish, meat and poultry dishes is unrivalled. Traditional snail dishes vary throughout the area. The great fish stews, really soups, are *bourride*, composed of white fish in a garlic mayonnaise sauce (*aioli*) – *aioli* is also the name of a Provençal cod-fish dish with vegetables in this garlic sauce – and *bouillabaisse*, composed of small rock fish in garlic and olive oil. *Salade niçoise* includes cold boiled potatoes and runner beans, with anchovies, tomatoes and black olives. *Daube* is the Provençal red meat casserole in a thick sauce.

Normandy

Like Brittany, Normandy offers a selection of sea platters with shellfish, sole, turbot and ray in particular, prepared in a variety of ways. Cream and butter take preference over olive oil as the bases for sauces which are part of meat and fish dishes. A lot of British palates will appreciate the Viré black-pudding sausage and Caen tripe served with vegetables in a cider sauce. Farmhouse cooking is the general style rather than fine *cuisine.*

The South-West, Languedoc and the Pyrenees

Home to the best goose-liver pâté – but don't watch how geese are fed up for this delicacy – the area is considered to offer the healthiest food in France, despite the rich, fatty content of renowned dishes like *cassoulet* (white beans, with pork and/or sausage in a thick sauce) which hails mainly from Carcassonne and Toulouse. Tripe is not Normandy's prerogative and *le gras double*, spicy tripe, ham and vegetable stew, is an Albi speciality. Prunes from Agen are used to season meat and game dishes. Catalan sausage and grilled snails are Pyrenean specialities. Tunny (*thon*) and sardines are caught on the Atlantic coast. Try peppered tuna steaks (*steak de thon pané aux poivres*).

Useful vocabulary

The vocabulary list which follows contains mainly fruit and vegetables which are encountered in regional menu cards; food that you may not come across when shopping at home, even if you live in France. The list also attempts to translate some unusual cooking terms and *cuisine* methods so that a speciality dish when it is served does not come as a total surprise.

airelle	bilberry
araignée	spider crab
agneau cuit sept heures	lamb, roasted for seven hours; advance orders probable
baekenofe	pot-roast dish
carpaccio	thinly sliced chilled raw meat or fish in olive oil and lemon juice
brandade de morue	oven baked cod and potato pie
canette	duckling; also a small bottle or can of beer
cèpe	cep (brown-capped mushroom)
chanterelle	chanterelle (yellow funnel-shaped mushroom, apricot flavoured)

girolle	another name for chanterelle mushrooms
morille	morel (brown, honeycombed cap mushroom)
garbure	a slowly steamed dish
gougeonnettes	cut into strips or fingers
kaki	persimmon (orange tomato-like fruit: very sweet and fleshy)
laurier	sweet bay (leaf)
nèfle	medlar (small apple-like fruit)
pain perdu	bread pudding
piment	chilli
piquillos	mild peppers
quasi	upper leg cut of veal
raifort	horseradish
trilogie de veau	veal fillet with veal pancreas and veal kidneys in equal portions

Useful Vocabulary

Some False Friends

French	Meaning	Possibly confused with
actuellement	at present, nowadays	actually
agenda	diary	agenda
blouse	overall, smock	blouse
brassière	baby's vest, life-jacket	brassiere
brasserie	pub	brassiere
cabinet	toilet, surgery, agency, office	cabinet
car	coach, bus, van	car
caution	guarantee, bail	caution
cave	cellar, wine retailer	cave
cellier	storeroom	cellar
chips	potato crisps	chips
collège	secondary school	college
conducteur	driver, guide	conductor
conférence	lecture	conference
déception	disappointment	deception
éditer	to publish	to edit

éventuellement	possibly	eventually
formellement	positively, definitely	formally
herbe	grass	herb
ignorer	to not know, to be unaware of	to ignore
inhabité	uninhabited	inhabited
large	wide	large
libraire	bookseller	library or librarian
location	renting, reservation	location
massif/ve	solid	massive
passer un examen	to take/sit an exam	to pass an exam
pétrôle	oil, petroleum	petrol
photographe	photographer	photograph
porc	pig, pigskin	pork
préservatif	contraceptive	preservative
professeur	teacher, master	professor
prune	plum	prune
radio	x-ray	radio
raisin	grape	raisin
relation	relationship, acquaintance	relation
répertoire	index notebook, alphabetical list	repertoire
route	road	route
scotch	Sellotape	Scotch whisky
sensible	sensitive	sensible
spectacle	theatrical show, entertainment	spectacle
standing	luxury, de luxe (buildings)	standing (status or position)
starter	car choke	starter (in car)
terrible	fantastic, great	terrible
veste	jacket	vest

UNESCO World Heritage Cultural and Natural Sites in France

- Mont-Saint-Michel and its bay. The church on the summit dates from the eleventh and twelfth centuries.

- Chartres Cathedral. Glorious medieval architecture, superb twelfth and thirteenth century stained-glass windows.

- Louis XIV's enormous Versailles Palace and its grounds laid out *à la française*.

- Vézela's Roman basilica and church, an important medieval pilgrimage destination.

- Ancient grottos in the Vézère valley (Dordogne).

- Fontainebleau: the Renaissance Château and formal gardens.

- Amiens Cathedral. Gothic splendour (Arundel Cathedral in Sussex, England is a copy).

- Orange. The Roman theatre, surrounds and triumphal arch.

- Arles. Roman buildings and remains (church, baths, amphitheatre, etc).

- Fontenay's (Burgundy) twelfth century Cistercian Abbey.

- Former eighteenth century royal salt-works at Arc-et-Senans (Doubs).

- Nancy. Historic old town (some restoration work may be in progress).

- Saint-Savin-sur-Gartempe (Vienne): the Abbey's collection of Roman murals.

- Gorolata and Porto headlands, Scandola nature reserve and the Piana inlets, in Corsica.

- Pont du Gard Roman aqueduct. The most popular ancient site in France.

- Strasbourg: the *grand île*.

- Paris: Seine banks, including Iles de la Cité and St Louis.

- Rheims Notre Dame Cathedral, the Saint-Rémi Abbey and the Tau palace.

- Bourges Gothic Cathedral with remarkable acoustics.

- Avignon historic town centre: the Papal city.

- The Canal du Midi, the hand-dug 240 km canal stretching from Toulouse to Béziers.

- The old fortified area of Carcassonne. Perhaps the best preserved fortress in Europe.

- The Chemin de Saint-Jacques-de-Compostelle (GR 65). The medieval pilgrims' route running from Aubrac (south Auvergne) to north-west Spain.

- Lyon historic centre.

- Saint-Emilion area (*juridiction*): seventh century hermitage, underground chapel.

- The Loire valley château country between Sully-sur-Loire (Loiret) and Chalonnes-sur-Loire (Maine et Loire).

- Provins: originally a Roman site, now famous for its roses and medieval monuments.

Further Reading

Books

A.A. France – Bed and Breakfast. The Automobile Association.

A.A. France – Caravanning, Camping. The Automobile Association.

The French, Theodore Zeldin. Fontana.

The Best Places to Buy a Home in France, Joe Laredo. Survival Books.

Hugh Johnson's Pocket Wine Book, Hugh Johnson. Mitchell Beazley. French edition, Flammarion.

Complete Atlas of Wine, Hugh Johnson. Mitchell Beazley.

French Cheeses. Dorling Kindersley.

French Wines, Robert Joseph. Dorling Kindersley.

Michelin Hotels & Restaurants Guide with explanations to symbols in English. Michelin.

Michelin Camping France with explanations to symbols in English. Michelin.

Rough Guide to Hotels and Restaurants in France. Rough Guides, in association with *Le Guide du Routard*.

Les Meilleurs Restaurants/Best Restaurants – Provence Côte d'Azur. Guide Horus (SARL Intermedia).

Les Plus Beaux Détours en France. Free guide with introduction in English, 81 lovely little towns throughout France. Write to Les Plus Beaux Détours de France, 26, rue de l'Etoile, 75017 Paris. See also Useful Websites.

English language newspapers and magazines

The News, SARL Brussac, 225 route d'Angoulème, BP 4042, 24004 Perigueux, France. National/regional news 'for residents and lovers of France'. Classified ads. Monthly.

The Connexion, BP 25, 06480 la colle sur Loup, France. Mainly national news 'for English-speakers living in and visiting France'. Classified ads. Monthly.

The Riviera Times, 8 avenue Jean Moulin, 06340 Drap, France. Local and national news. Classified ads. Monthly.

Focus on France, Outbound Publishing, 1 Commercial Road, Eastbourne, East Sussex BN21 3XQ. Property information, articles and advertisements. Every two months.

French Property Magazine, 6 Burgess Mews, Wimbledon, London SW19 1UF. Property information, articles and advertisements. Monthly.

Books in Franglais

Ciel! Blake! (Dictionnaire Français-Anglais des Expressions Courantes), Jean-Loup Chiflet. Mots & Cie.

Sky My Husband! Ciel Mon Mari!, Jean-Loup Chiflet. Seuil.

Sky My Husband II! The Return, Jean-Loup Chiflet. Hermé.

Sky My Wife! Ciel Ma Femme!, Jean-Loup Chiflet. Seuil.

Books in French

Les Carnets du Major Thompson, Pierre Daninois. Livre de Poche.

Le Major Tricolore, Pierre Daninois. Hachette.

Nos Meilleurs Chambres d'Hotes en France. Guide Routard.

French magazines

L'Express. Weekly. Publishes every autumn a special property issue giving prices for property sales throughout France.

Le Point. Weekly. Publishes beginning of every year their list of the best towns in which to live in France.

Useful Websites

General, home improvements, food

www.aeroport.fr
Flights to and from major airports in France plus information on all other French airports etc.

www.lepoint.fr
Le Point magazine's website has a league table in French, updated every January, of the best 100 towns in which to live.

www.tgv.com
Plan your journey and book your seat on the high-speed train service.

www.britishcouncil.org/anglophone-schools-in-france.pdf
Schools in France with teaching in English.

www.bbc.co.uk
Keep up-to-date with UK news.

www.angloinfo.com
Where to learn French in Britanny, Normandy and south-east France.

www.education.gouv.fr
Up-to-date information from the Ministry of Education covering primary school to university. Includes section for foreign students wishing to pursue higher education courses in France.

www.legifrance.gouv.fr
French law (*le droit français*) in English. Also visit *dossiers législatifs* – only in French – for recent and forthcoming laws.

www.argusauto.com
The website of the weekly magazine *L'argus de l'automobile*. Apart from secondhand car prices, it includes a schedule of acceptable repair job prices and new car model prices and features.

www.castorama.fr
Prices and details (in French only) of all their DIY and garden products and building materials. Online ordering.

www.leroymerlin.fr
Prices and details (in French only) of all their DIY and garden products and building materials. Comparison of their similar products. Online ordering.

www.lapeyre.fr
Prices and details of their home improvement products. Online ordering in French and English.

www.salon-agriculture.com
Details, now in English of the International Paris Agricultural show. All the best in dairy farming, live-stock breeding and wine production.

www.foire-de-paris.com
In French. All about the Paris general, home, garden and leisure exhibition.

www.guideduvin.org
Advice and general information on what wine to choose, how to serve and how to store, with a section in English.

www.champagnedirect.com
Selected champagnes for online purchase, but not directly from the producers. In French.

www.bestofbritish.fr
British food (Marmite etc) online ordering.

www.casino.fr
All about the casino retail group including eating in their restaurants. In English.

www.bocuse.com/us/restaurant
Paul Bocuse, one of the greatest French chefs, reveals all about his recipes – the translations are poor. Recipe creations online.

www.epicuria.fr
French only. Regional recipes, restaurant and hotel bookings, and gastronomic shopping online.

Retirement, statistics, phone services

www.insee.fr
National website full of facts and figures on the French economy and society. English version.

www.francetelecom.fr
International website in English of 'one of the world's leading telecommunications carriers'.
Free phone services, *mes services compris* in the French section, *votre agence en ligne*, such as answerphone (*messagerie vocale*), which number called, dial 3131 and ex-directory (*liste rouge*).

www.pagesjaunes.fr
French *Yellow Pages* online.

www.budgetelecom.com
In French only. Compare prices between the various land-line and mobile-phone operators, and also between the various internet online service companies. N.B. Split

your phone bill into types of calls for simulated on-screen comparisons.

www.retraites.gouv.fr
In French only. Questions and answers on understanding and preparing for retirement following the 2003 retirement law changes.

Holidays, leisure

www.abritel.fr
Private homes for holiday rentals.

www.bison-fute.equipement.gouv.fr
Practical information on road traffic conditions.

www.campingfrance.com
English information on some camping sites.

www.plusbeauxdetours.com
English descriptions of 81 charming little towns to visit scattered all over France.

www.salon-vehicules-loisirs.com
All about the Paris motor home show. In English.

www.chateauversailles.fr
Comprehensive information in English.

www.chateaux-france.com
Detailed information in English on châteaux throughout France offering accommodation and/or which can be visited.

www.gaf.tm.fr
Camping sites, hotels, gîtes etc throughout France.

www.thegoodbookguide.com
The best of British books by mail order.

www.vvf-vacances.fr

The *village vacances* (holiday camps) website.

www.quelleroute.com
Route planning site.

www.voyages-sncf.com
Holiday deals incorporating rail travel.

www.webhomeexchange.com
Homes available for holiday exchanges.

www.homelink.org
Homes available for holiday exchanges.

www.inffni.org
The International Naturist Federation website, in English, with link to the French national federation site **www.ffn-naturisme.com** (in French only).

www.fr.lastminute.com/fr
Short notice reduced price holidays.

www.degriftour.fr
Short notice reduced price holidays.

www.parcs-naturels-regionaux.tm.fr
Guide to the 42 regional nature parks with some parts in English.

Property

www.french-property-news.com
Properties for sale details online. Magazine subscription details.

www.worldofpropertyexhibition.com
Properties for sale details online. *Focus on France* magazine subscription details.

www.fnaim.com
The website, in French only, of the National Federation of Estate Agents (FNAIM), showing their members throughout France.

www.immonot.com
Conveyancing costs under *frais de notaires* on the French notaries' information site.

www.immoprix.com
French notaries' survey throughout France of prices paid in the previous year for old and new houses and flats, and building land.

Employment

www.anpe.fr and **www.apec.fr**
Thousands of jobs always listed on the national employment agency general and managerial sites. Pre-selection email advice systems.

www.travail.gouv.fr/english
Up-to-date information in English from the Ministry of Employment.

www.100cv.com
Contains over 100 examples of CVs using Word, 50 CVs for website creation and 50 all important *lettres de motivation*. Translations from French. A UK phone call to obtain access code for services costs £1.50.

Index